BUTTERFLIES & MOTHS
IN BRITAIN

This Work is a Volume in

THE BRITISH NATURE LIBRARY

A series of volumes on the different aspects
of Natural History in the British Isles,
each written by an expert and illustrated
by one or more colour plates and 100
of the best nature photographs available.
The colour jackets of the first three
volumes are by John Nash

Demy 8vo   10s. 6d. net each

WILD ANIMALS IN BRITAIN

By FRANCES PITT. Second Edition

WILD BIRDS IN BRITAIN

By SETON GORDON. Second Edition

WILD FLOWERS IN BRITAIN

By ROBERT GATHORNE-HARDY: with 4 coloured
lithographs and numerous line drawings by John
Nash. Second Edition

PUBLISHED BY

B. T. BATSFORD, LTD.

15, NORTH AUDLEY STREET LONDON, W.1
AND MALVERN WELLS, WORCESTERSHIRE

PLATE I.

Top left: PEACOCK.   *Top right:* WHITE ADMIRAL.   *Middle left:* RED ADMIRAL.   *Middle right:* PAINTED LADY.   *Lower left corner:* SMALL TORTOISESHELL AND CHRYSALIS.   *Lower right corner:* PAINTED LADY, WITH RED ADMIRAL'S CHRYSALIS JUST ABOVE IT.

THE BRITISH NATURE LIBRARY

BUTTERFLIES AND MOTHS
IN BRITAIN

By
VERE TEMPLE

*With 10 Lithographic Plates in colour, and 57 Drawings
in the Text by the Author, together with 95
Photographic Reproductions*

LONDON
B. T. BATSFORD, LIMITED
15 North Audley Street, Mayfair, W. 1
and Malvern Wells, Worcestershire

First published, Winter, 1945–6

To
DORA ILSE

MADE AND PRINTED IN GREAT BRITAIN
FOR THE PUBLISHERS, B. T. BATSFORD, LTD.
BY JARROLD AND SONS, LTD., NORWICH

PREFACE AND
AUTHOR'S ACKNOWLEDGMENT

IN this book I have described butterflies and moths that I know, and I have written of the countryside that is their setting. But since our delight in the contemplation of Nature is increased by knowledge, I have added a spice of information to my descriptions. Here my debt to others is great.

I am particularly indebted to L. W. Newman, Esq., late F.R.E.S., and to L. Hugh Newman, Esq., F.R.E.S., for their kindness in putting at my disposal their great knowledge and practical experience of moths and butterflies. I should also like to thank Dr. C. B. Williams, Chief Entomologist at Rothamsted Experimental Station, who has provided me with material for my notes on the migration of butterflies and of moths.

For scientific information I am also indebted to Dr. D. Ilse, who has imparted to me the gist of her recent observations on the "drumming" of female butterflies. Further experiments made by her with regard to the colour-sense of butterflies have recently been published in *Nature* and a summary of them has been given to me by Dr. A. D. Imms, of Cambridge University. N. D. Riley, Esq., F.R.E.S., Editor of the *Entomologist* and Keeper of Entomology at the British Museum (Natural History), has enlightened me with regard to various other scientific details.

My thanks are due to H. M. Edelsten, Esq., and to A. G. Gabriel, Esq., who have given me access to books in the Natural History Museum.

I have also gleaned useful information from the following books:

The Text-book of British Butterflies and Moths, by L. W. Newman, and H. A. Leeds. (Giles & Bamforth, Ltd.)

Butterflies and Moths of the Wayside and Woodland, compiled by W. J. Stokoe. (Frederick Warne & Co., Ltd.)

Butterfly Lore, by Dr. H. Eltringham. (Clarendon Press.)

Butterflies and Moths of the British Isles, by Richard South. (Frederick Warne & Co., Ltd.)

Butterflies and Moths at home and abroad, by H. Rowland Brown. (Ernest Benn.)

The Migration of Butterflies, by C. B. Williams. (Oliver & Boyd.)

Butterflies and Moths of the Countryside, by Edward Hulme. (Hutchinson, Ltd.)

Natural History of British Butterflies, by F. W. Frohawk. (Hutchinson, Ltd.)

Nature Parade, by Frank Lane. (Jarrolds.)

The Life of the Caterpillar, by J. H. Fabre. (Hodder & Stoughton.)

The Life of the Butterfly, by Friedrich Schnack.

Insect Behaviour, by Evelyn Cheesman. (Phillip Allan & Co.)

The Colour Vision of Insects, by Dora Ilse, reprint from the Proceedings of the Royal Philosophical Society of Glasgow, for the 139th and 140th sessions. 1940–1941 and 1941–1942. Vol. LXV, published by the Society, 207 Bath Street, 1941.

Principles of Insect Physiology, by V. B. Wigglesworth. (Methuen.)

Biologie der Schmetterlinge, by Dr. Martin Hering—Biologische Studien-bücher III, achtes Kapitel—Liebespiel und Begattung, published by J. Springer, Berlin, 1926.

———

I have throughout this book given both the English and the Latin names of the Butterflies and Moths. I have used the generic and specific names given in W. J. Stokoe's *Butterflies and Moths of the Wayside and Woodland*, 1939, which accord with the international rules of zoological nomenclature. N. D. Riley, Esq., Keeper of Entomology at the British Museum (Natural History) has kindly brought the nomenclature up to date (July 1945).

Space did not allow me to mention, in the text, various moths, eggs and caterpillars depicted in the photographic plates. These are:

eggs of Pale Prominent moth, *Pterostoma palpina* (58).

  ,,   Silver Cloud moth, *Xylomiges conspicillaris* (60).

  ,,   Sweet Gate moth, *Apatele euphorbiae* var. *myricae* (66).

  ,,   Common Marbled Carpet moth, *Dysstroma truncata* (94).

  ,,   Scarce Tissue moth, *Calocalpa cervinalus* (91).

caterpillar of moths December moth, *Poecilocampa populi* (80).

  ,,   ,,   Treble-bar moth, *Anaitis plagiata* (83) and Plate IX.

  ,,   ,,   Broken-barred Carpet moth, *Electrophaes coryolata* (82).

  ,,   ,,   Dotted Border moth, *Erannis marginaria* (85).

The caterpillars of the Marsh Fritillary and of the Isle of Wight Fritillary, and the chrysalises of the Marsh Fritillary, depicted in Plate III. are enlarged in order to show their construction. The male Emperor moth in Plate X is also slightly enlarged.

VERE TEMPLE

ACKNOWLEDGMENT

The Publishers have pleasure in recording their thanks to the undermentioned for permission to reproduce the subjects as indicated:

Pentland Hick, 46; Dr. Dora Ilse, 1, 8, 9, 12, 13, 36, 48; E. F. Linssen, A.R.P.S., and L. Hugh Newman, F.R.E.S., 11, 14, 15, 19, 20, 21, 25, 26, 30, 31, 32, 33, 35, 44, 45, 51, 52, 53, 55, 56, 57, 65, 69, 73, 74, 78, 81; Walter J. C. Murray, 10, 16, 17, 22, 23, 34, 40, 41, 42, 43, 49, 50, 70, 71, 72, 77, 95; L. Hugh Newman, F.R.E.S., 2, 3, 4, 5, 18, 24, 29, 37, 46, 54, 61, 62, 63, 64, 75, 76, 79, 80, 82, 83, 84, 85, 86, 87, 88, 89, 90; Mrs. Tonge and Beowolf Cooper, 6, 7, 27, 28, 38, 39, 47, 58, 59, 60, 66, 67, 68, 91, 92, 93, 94; D. Wilbrandt, 8, 9.

To Messrs. Frederick Warne and Co., Ltd., for the illustration on page 4 from *The Butterflies of the British Isles*.

The colour plates and drawings in the text are by the author. The subjects in colour used for the jacket design have been slightly enlarged.

CONTENTS

PART I—BUTTERFLIES

CHAPTER   PAGE

PREFACE AND AUTHOR'S ACKNOWLEDGMENT   v

PUBLISHERS' ACKNOWLEDGMENT   vii

I. INTRODUCTORY   1

II. SPRING   5

III. MIGRANTS AND OTHERS   12

IV. THE FOREST   19

V. THE FENS   22

VI. THE DOWNS   25

VII. HEDGEROW AND HILLSIDE   30

VIII. THE WOODLANDS   36

IX. GREY DAYS: SOME NOTES ON THE COURTSHIP
OF BUTTERFLIES   43

X. AUTUMN   53

PART II—MOTHS

XI. MOTHS   59

XII. HAWK-MOTHS (*Sphingidae*)   63

XIII. THE PROMINENTS (*Notodontidae*) AND TUSSOCKS
(*Lymantriidae*)   70

XIV. THE NOCTUIDS (*Noctuidae*)   78

XV. THE EMPEROR (*Saturniidae*), THE EGGARS (*Lasiocampidae*),
TIGERS (*Arctiinae*) AND FOOTMEN (*Lithosiinae*)   87

XVI. THE GEOMETERS (*Geometridae*)   97

XVII. PRIMITIVE MOTHS AND TREE-BORING CATER-
PILLARS (*Cossidae, Sesiidae* and *Hepialidae*)   103

PART III

XVIII. NOTES ON COLLECTING, SETTING AND STORING
BUTTERFLIES AND MOTHS   107

INDEX   117

PART I   BUTTERFLIES

CHAPTER I

Introductory

A YOUNG friend said to me the other day: "I've found a butterfly for you. It's not very big, so I think it must be a young one. I squashed it, in case it might eat my clothes." And he produced, from a matchbox, the battered remains of a Yellow Underwing moth.

Now, there is still hope for my friend's ultimate entomological salvation, for he is but seven years old; but in case similar fallacies prevail among my readers, I think I had better give them, at the outset of this book and as concisely as possible, the ABC of the science of entomology.

First then: butterflies and moths never grow. Their growing, and most of their eating, is all done in the caterpillar stage, when their gastronomic feats are surprising. A caterpillar eats many times its own weight in green leaves; it spends its whole life either eating (sometimes beginning with the shell of the egg from which it hatched), or digesting food, or, at intervals, sloughing, and sometimes eating its skin, which an inordinate appetite has made uncomfortably tight. When, full-grown and replete, it can eat no more, it seeks some secluded corner, there to undergo a transformation into its third mummy-like state of pupa or chrysalis,[1] from which, in due course, the perfect insect emerges. When the newly hatched butterfly or moth crawls from its pupa, its wings are small and soft, folded many-wise on themselves like accordion-pleating; but the new-born insect, clinging to chrysalis-shell or branch, pumps liquid from its body through the nervures (much as one inflates a bicycle-tyre) so that the wings are soon expanded to their full extent.

Secondly: butterflies and moths, having no jaws, but only a proboscis or tongue (and in at least one family of moths, not even that), can imbibe nothing more solid than the nectar from flowers, and a little dew.

How can you tell a butterfly from a moth?

The butterfly invariably flies by day, and the moth usually by night; but as there are quite a number of moths who are day-fliers, it is best to rely on another difference, namely, that the butterfly has knobs on the tips of its antennæ. In the moth, these antennæ are either thread-like, or thickened at the base, thence tapering to a point; or else they are toothed, or fringed. In the "Skippers", those queer little butterflies that are the

---

[1] The word chrysalis is derived from the Greek "Chrusos", gold, descriptive of the "gilding" apparent in some species; that of pupa from the Latin word for a little doll.

connecting link between butterflies and moths, the antennæ are slightly
thickened at the tip. There is also one family of moths with clubbed
antennæ: the red and black Burnets, that fly in the sunshine.

There is yet another difference between butterflies and moths.

You will find the naked and angular chrysalis of the butterfly either
suspended from, or lashed to, its support. The pupa of the moth, which
is smooth and puppet-like, is in some species enclosed in a cocoon, which
the caterpillar spins round itself before sloughing its last skin; while
others burrow into the ground, where they hollow out a cavity, whose
walls they harden with a special secretion. In this tomb they await their
resurrection. The Skipper butterflies here again effect a compromise,
and weave, round their chrysalis, a rudimentary cocoon.

Some kinds of caterpillars hatch from eggs laid on the leaves of their
food-plants, and are thus surrounded by plenty from the first. But there
are various species of moths that lay their eggs on the bark of the tree,
and the newly hatched caterpillars have to crawl some distance to find
their food. Experiments made with one such species prove that the young
caterpillars will always crawl towards the light. In their wild state, this
naturally comes from above, and guides them to the tips of the twigs
where their food awaits them. The scent of the leaves now becomes the
guiding instinct, and the caterpillar feeds.

Its tiny eyes are probably not of much use to the caterpillar which appears
to depend for guidance on two antennæ, or feelers, so small as to be
invisible to the naked eye.

The anatomy of the caterpillar is well adapted to the assimilation of
food. The mandibles, or jaws, with which it eats, work sideways, like
pincers, or scissors; an upper and a lower lip help down the mouthfuls,
which pass into a large and active digestive tract. The caterpillar wears
its rudimentary heart, not on his sleeve, but along its back, in the form of a
pulsating cord that keeps its "blood" in motion. It has almost four
times as many muscles as a man, but no veins or arteries; its "blood"
runs free, and its nervous system is distributed at intervals along its body.
(As its sensations probably centre upon food, this proximity of nerve
centres and stomach certainly seems a logical arrangement.) The small
apertures that you will observe at the sides of each of its twelve or thirteen
segments are spiracles, or breathing holes, admitting air to an inner network of tubes.

In addition to its six "true" front legs—which reappear in the perfect
insect—the caterpillar possesses four pairs of "claspers" or prolegs,
arranged under its hinder segments, and an additional one under the last
segment of all. With these it walks, and their sucker-like pads enable it
to cling firmly to its food-plant whilst feeding or at rest. Most caterpillars
bear on their heads a spinneret, connected to an inner sac containing liquid
silk, which hardens to a thread when drawn out. This is the material
used for the yellow and white floss silk of the silkworm, for the rougher

cocoons and glue-lined pupal cases of other moths, and for the tail-pads and girdles of silk that suspend some chrysalises.

A vestige of the proboscis of the future insect is apparent as a pair of tiny maxillæ, one on each side of the lower lip, but there is as yet no sign of the wings. These appear at the beginning of the pupal stage.

Earthbound and hungry, the caterpillar eats its way through this stage of its existence; a lowly enough creature, yet perhaps surprising to those of you who have hitherto looked upon caterpillars as being "nothing but skin and squash".

But when the butterfly bursts from its pupal prison, what a trans-formation we behold! The hard flat head is now elongated and downy, equipped with large compound eyes, antennæ of the most delicate structure, and a complicated nervous system from which subsidiary nerves run the length of the insect's body. The mouth parts have changed from horny jaws to a slender proboscis, sometimes as much as four inches in length, which lies coiled on itself like a watchspring when not in use. Two hairy, forward-pointing palpi above the mouthparts are believed to be organs of taste.

It is now generally agreed that the antennæ are the organs of smell and of balance. They are, however, covered with a large number of tiny sense organs of varying kinds, with no doubt, varying purposes. The antennæ each contain a central nerve-cord, connecting with the brain.

The sight of a butterfly differs from ours in that it consists of a kind of mosaic picture, each fragment formed by one of the thousands of lenses of the compound eye, to which only objects close at hand are clearly visible.

The thorax, or part of the body behind the head, is the muscular centre and bears six legs and four wings. Each leg has four parts—the basal joint, the thigh, the shank and the foot, which last consists of four joints ending in a claw. The feet are equipped with sense-organs. The wing consists of an upper and a lower layer of membrane, stretched between a framework of hollow tubes, which act as supporting ribs. These are known as "veins" or "nervures" (a misleading name as they have nothing to do with nerves).

If you now examine these lovely wings through a lens, you will see that their coloured dust, that rubs off so easily, is composed of innumerable flat scales, arranged in lines on short stalks that fit into sockets in the membrane of the wing, upon which they overlap like the feathers of a bird, or like tiles upon a roof. Male butterflies are distinguished by elaborate scales known as "androconia", which are diversely shaped, some being like fans, others like feathers, or boat paddles, or battledores; whilst others again are cleft and divided, like the fingers of an outspread hand. The wings of many male butterflies bear, also, scent-scales, the function of which is to attract the female butterfly.

The third, or hindmost part of the body, the abdomen, contains the digestive and generative organs. Like the caterpillar, the butterfly carries its heart along his back, its blood runs free, it breathes through spiracles that convey the air to every part of his body.

Butterflies and moths form one of the great natural orders of insects —the Lepidoptera (scale wings). The shape of their antennæ gives to butterflies their name of Rhopalocera (club-horns) and to moths that of Heterocera (horns otherwise arranged).

There are to be found in Britain sixty-eight kinds of butterflies (of which eleven are migrants), and more than two thousand kinds of moths. Let us now go out into the countryside, and find some of them.

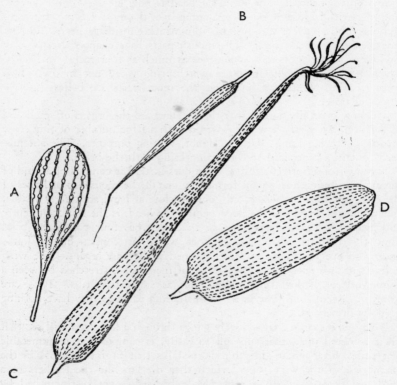

ANDROCONIA OR PLUMULES (WING SCALES)

A. Bladder Plumule (Common Blue)
B. Bristle Plumule (Grizzled Skipper)
C. Tufted Plumule (Satyrs)
D. Dotted Plumule (White-letter Hairstreak)

1   Small Tortoiseshell Butterfly. *Aglais urticae*, laying eggs on Stinging-nettle

[*Magnification* × 2½

3 The Caterpillar's last skin is shed, disclosing the Chrysalis

[Slightly larger than life

2 Caterpillar "spun up" with silken girdle, ready to turn into a Chrysalis

[Slightly larger than life

Life History of the Brimstone Butterfly, *Gonepteryx rhamni*

CHAPTER II

Spring

I INTEND to write about moths in the second part of this book. To enliven the first part, I will take you for a holiday, in search of butterflies, round the countryside of Britain. And if you are the sort of person who enjoys Nature in retrospect, you will, I hope, for ever remember with delight that holiday; long days in the July woods, where fritillaries float across glades all starred with yellow tormentil and wild strawberry; lazy afternoons in a garden, where Red Admirals and Peacocks strut and flaunt on the buddleia blossoms in the mellow September sunshine; or a cliff-top, peopled by a colony of that most confiding of all moths, the Six-spot Burnet; sea-gulls crying, and, far below, the blue and whispering sea.

Not having a magic carpet to transport us, we will travel in a motor-caravan. Thus we can hurry through areas where there are no butterflies, halting in more favoured places where beauties abound. And, if it is on collecting that you are bent, do not let us forget to stock the shelves and cupboards of our caravan with the microscope, butterfly net, entomological forceps, setting-boards, pill-boxes, killing-bottle and all the other paraphernalia of our hobby (Chapter XVIII).

We must also take note-books, pencils and drawing-paper; for if I succeed in firing you with my enthusiasm, you will, I hope, be anxious to record your own observations. With these resources, and the cooking to do, we shall not feel dull on wet days. But let us hope that the sun, and fortune, will smile upon our holiday.

We will start in Kent (a happy hunting-ground of the entomologist, particularly of the moth-hunter). The climate here is warm, and coaxes out, early in the year, the butterflies that hibernate.

With what joy, after a winter in town, do we escape into the April countryside! Thrills of pleasure run through us as we sniff the warm earthy smells of early spring and the scent of the first white violets. Above, the beech-buds are fat against the blue sky, they emit faint crackling noises as their scales expand in the sun. I can hear a stirring in the ground, as the growing things push their way upwards through the carpet of last year's fallen leaves. And here, thankfully, sunning itself, like us, after a winter indoors, there sits, on the bare ground, a Small Tortoiseshell butterfly, *Aglais urticae* (Frontispiece, Plate I and 1). Chips are torn from its wings and its colours are dimmed, yet to me it is a lovely sight, for it is a sign of spring.

I love this tawny butterfly for its beauty as well as for the sake of pleasant associations; for when, with colours untarnished, its children reappear,

2*   5

newly hatched, in June or August, their black and tawny wings beaded with turquoise are by no means unworthy of the family of beauties of which they are the commonest members. The romance of travel surrounds their relations, the Red Admiral, *Vanessa atalanta* (Frontispiece, Plate I), and the Painted Lady, *Vanessa cardui* (Frontispiece, Plate I), for they are spring migrants from the Continent. I shall write about them later and with enthusiasm.

Caterpillars of Small Tortoiseshell Butterfly, *Aglais urticae*
Sunning themselves on their web
(*Life-size*)

The Small Tortoiseshell (Frontispiece, Plate I and 1) hibernates throughout the cold months in sheltered corners—hollow trees, outhouses, or barns—and emerges in March and mates, and in April lays eggs which become June and July butterflies. The offspring of this generation are the late summer Tortoiseshells, destined to survive the winter.

Like other butterflies of the same family, the Small Tortoiseshell walks with two pairs of legs. The first front pair are rudimentary and nestle in down close to the head. In the male these short legs have no joints and look like brushes covered with hairs. But in the female the legs are spiny and the joints are apparent.

Until recent observation on the subject, the real function of these rudimentary front legs had not been known, though Dr. Eltringham

Small Tortoiseshell, *Aglais urticae*, **Caterpillars on Nettle**
Showing web and cast skins
(*Life-size*)

found that they contain the same sense-organs that exist in the second
pair of legs, which are considered by one authority to be organs of taste.
Aglais urticae "drums" on nettles only, but other species of butterflies
will "drum" on various green plants and by doing so apparently recognise
whether they are the right kind: if the plant is unsuitable they immediately
fly off. Dr. Ilse has observed thus "drumming reaction" in seven species
of butterflies.

When the female Tortoiseshell is about to lay her eggs, she flies to a
patch of stinging-nettles, to which she is probably guided by her sense of
smell. On alighting, she tests the surface of the leaves by "drumming"
on them with these sensitive front legs. She then lays a batch of eggs—
anything from 50 to 200—in a tight cluster on the underside of the
topmost shoot where it looks like a swelling on the leaf (1). She lays several
other batches during her life and usually allots one batch to each plant,
so that there will be plenty of food for each company of caterpillars.

These are striped, spiny, ugly creatures. In their early stages they spin
a web, in which they lead a communal life. At night they huddle into the
protection of this web, which serves also as a shelter during rain, and as a
carpet on which to bask in the sunshine.

Let me here confess to an unentomological failing: the webs of caterpillars fill me with loathing. The only web that I can bring myself to
like and to admire, as a work of art, and as an engineering feat, and also
from the point of view of utility, is that of the Garden Spider. Perhaps
it is that I am a tidy person (I enjoy spring-cleaning) and that my house-
wifely heart is vexed at the sight of those hideous webs of the Lackey
Moth and others, that clutter up the nice green hedgerow. Perhaps it is
that I am an individualist, and that an innate hatred of crowds has its
entomological echoes. Whatever the reason, I prefer solitary caterpillars.
Who can remain unmoved by the lonely grandeur of a Poplar Hawk, as
he sits, like some jade idol, withdrawn in meditation, on his twig? But
with regard to the Tortoiseshell, I'll admit that, like many young people,
he becomes more self-sufficient with maturity. He soon acquires a leaf
all to himself; and by and by you see him straying from his companions
to some safe nook or cranny, where he hangs himself up by a tail-pad of
silk. And presently, off comes his skin, revealing a pretty angular thing
resembling a crystal, or a pendant carved in marble: a chrysalis.[1]

If you examine it, you will see that the hinder legs of the caterpillar
have disappeared, though the six front ones remain, encased in a sheath,
and that the lower part of the body has assumed the pointed shape of a
butterfly. A double row of studs marks the position of the spiracles of
the caterpillar. The thorax is protected by armour, and rudimentary
wings are visible beneath swaddling bands, which enwrap also the proboscis
of the future insect. Now these are entirely new structures, not resembling

---

[1] The chrysalises of Tortoiseshells vary very much in colour. Sometimes they are
gilded, sometimes greenish-brown, and sometimes a dark, mottled brown.

Life History of the Brimstone Butterfly, *Gonepteryx rhamni*

4 The Butterfly has emerged from the Chrysalis,
   after a period of about ten days
   [*Life-size*]

5 The Butterfly flutters to the top of the spike of Buckthorn,
   where this transformation has taken place
   [*Magnification about* × 1⅜]

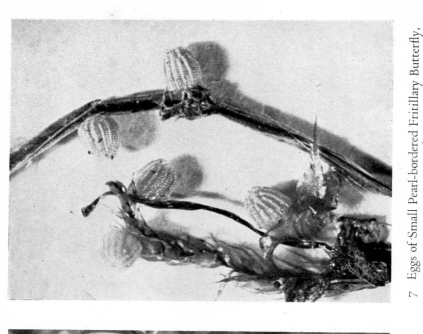

6 Eggs of Peacock Butterfly, *Nymphalis io*

Magnification × 40

COLOUR: OLIVE GREEN

7 Eggs of Small Pearl-bordered Fritillary Butterfly,
Argynnis selene

[*Magnification* × 25

COLOUR: PALE GREENISH YELLOW

anything to be found in the caterpillar. At the end of its development its tissues melt into a creamy liquid, and out of this the miracle is wrought. You will have noticed the twitchings of a caterpillar about to undergo transformation. That it is uncomfortable is evident, though not surprising, since it is in the throes of a living dissolution.

The newly hatched butterfly clings to the shell of its chrysalis. Its wings, small and crumpled at birth, have expanded, and are pressed together in all their downy perfection. The antennæ, bent forward above round eyes, give the head the appearance of that of a tiny deer. The fluffy face wears an expression of immemorial wisdom. Motionless, the newborn one rests awhile, gathering strength for its flight into the unknown.

Another sleeper has awakened to charm us with transitory beauty—the Brimstone, *Gonepteryx rhamni* (2, 3, 4, 5). Its leaf-shaped wings, sulphur-yellow in the male and greenish-white in the female, bear each a central orange dot and are downed above with silver, and, beneath, veined and green-tinted, so that the resting butterfly becomes one with leaves of the tree.

Small Tortoiseshell, *Aglais urticae*, Chrysalises
(*Life-size*)

This butterfly is one whose beauty to me familiarity cannot stale. I never tire of the pure curves of its wings. Appearing as it does with the pale spring sunshine, it is as if a primrose had taken flight. Ephemeral as it seems, the Brimstone is actually the longest-lived of all British butterflies, with the exception of the Small Tortoiseshell and its relations, the Peacock and the Comma, for it survives from August until the following May.

It seems as if the instincts of this butterfly retained memories of the short summer of an Ice Age; for it goes into hibernation as early as August. It can stand any amount of cold, and sleeps out of doors, choosing the protection of a bush, or a thicket of ivy, where it clings to a leaf with its strong, clawed feet. The males emerge first, and fly up and down, waiting for the awakening of their brides. It is said that they will pursue scraps of white paper fluttering in the breeze, mistaking them for female butterflies.

There is only one brood in the year. The eggs are laid singly on buckthorn leaves, and the caterpillars (2), which feed singly, are wonderfully disguised by their green colour and by a stripe, like the mid-rib of the leaf, down the middle of their bodies. In spite of their protective colouring they are, however, much subjected to the attacks of parasitic flies.

Eig' ty of these were seen to emerge from the chrysalis of a Brimstone
butterfly.

The chrysalis sleeps head upwards, slung to a branch by a silken thread

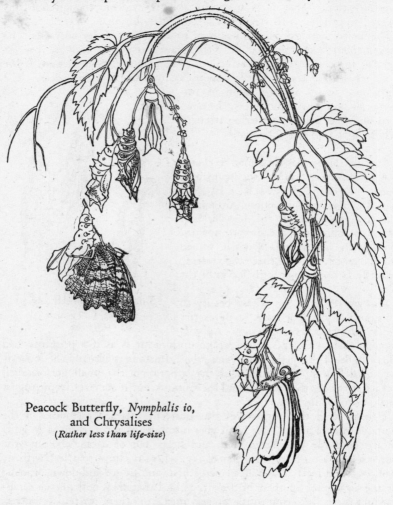

Peacock Butterfly, *Nymphalis io,*
and Chrysalises
(*Rather less than life-size*)

which the caterpillar (3), by a contortionist feat, ties round its middle
before transformation.

The Brimstone is the only English representative of a group hailing from
China and the Himalayas. A Continental variety, *Gonepteryx cleopatra,*
which I have seen in large numbers in the south of France, has the upper
surface of the forewings suffused with orange. Some years ago attempts

PLATE II.

Top left. CHRYSALISES OF ORANGE-TIP. *Top centre.* FEMALE ORANGE-TIP LAYING
EGGS ON FLOWER-CALYX OF HEDGE MUSTARD. *Top right.* CATERPILLAR OF ORANGE-
TIP. *Middle left.* SMALL WHITE. *Middle right.* FEMALE OF GREEN-VEINED WHITE
LAYING EGGS ON LEAF OF HEDGE-MUSTARD. *Centre.* ORANGE-TIP, MALE. *Lower
left.* CATERPILLARS AND CHRYSALIS OF SMALL WHITE. *Lower right.* GREEN-
VEINED WHITE, WITH OPEN WINGS. *Lower centre.* LARGE WHITE, FEMALE, WITH
CATERPILLAR AND CHRYSALIS BELOW. *Bottom right.* LARGE WHITE, MALE, DRYING
ITS WINGS.

were made to establish a colony of these butterflies in Ireland, but they disappeared after the third season.

Regarding the hibernating habits of the Tortoiseshell's handsome cousin, the Peacock, *Nymphalis io* (Frontispiece, Plate I, 8, 9), a naturalist relates how, one winter's day, he thrust his hand into a hollow tree, but withdrew it in haste, alarmed by a hissing sound. A closer inspection, however, revealed, not an adder, but an assembly of sleeping Peacocks. The friction of thei rdisturbed wings had produced the unexpected noise.[1]

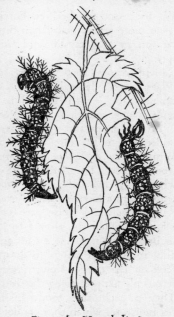

I have never had such an exciting experience as this, though I have often found the drowsy creatures, clinging to rafters in lofts, or behind a rolled-up blind. The splendour of their eyed wings seems slightly incongruous amid the pale flowers and east winds of spring. More rightly they adorn the passionate purple thistle-heads beneath a blazing August sun. The single-brooded Peacock caterpillars are black and spiny. Like the Tortoiseshell—and the Ancient Romans—they relish the nettle as food.

There are two other hibernating butterflies of this family, namely, the Comma, *Polygonia c-album* and the Large Tortoiseshell, *Nymphalis polychloros*; these are creatures of the late summer, as well as of the spring, and I shall write about them later.

Peacock, *Nymphalis io*,
Caterpillars on Nettle Leaf
(*Life-size*)

And now we must for a while content ourselves with the pleasures of anticipation, for it will be a fortnight or more before May, like Pandora, opens her casket of winged creatures—midges and gnats, and coarse-bodied flies as annoying to mankind as the evil sprites in the legend, and butterflies, rainbow-hued and beautiful as that other last imprisoned spirit—Hope. We have seen the three awakened sleepers that you may meet with on any country walk; the forest, the fen and the downland now await us, peopled by other butterflies whose lives are fraught with fantasy.

[1] It is scientifically known as stridulation.

CHAPTER III
Migrants and Others

WE are bound for the New Forest, but there is no need to hurry, for there is no more joyful place than Sussex on a May morning. Let us halt our caravan by the wayside and enjoy the sights and smells and sounds of spring.

Here comes that gay creature, *Euchloë cardamines*, the Orange-tip (Plate II, 10), flying low over the hedgerow plants. The male butterfly is unmistakable, with his white upper wings tipped with orange and under-wings mottled with green; but the female, exquisitely dressed in white, green and grey, bears a slight resemblance, especially on her underside, to the rare Bath White, formerly known as the Chequered White *Pontia daplidicae*, a continental butterfly which sometimes migrates from France. The Bath White was first observed in England near Bath, where a young lady, with commendable skill, worked on a piece of embroidery a likeness of this exciting "find".

The green and white garb of the female Orange-tip blends with the plant on which she alights to lay her eggs (Plate II); and when, feeling inclined for a nap, she settles among the mist of the cow-parsley, she has only to fold her wings to disappear from prying eyes. The caterpillars feed on the cuckoo-flower, hedge-mustard, wintercress and other cruciferous plants, preferring the seed-pods, which they resemble in appearance. They eat each other, too. This horrid habit is apparently due to a craving for moisture, which they cannot get from rain or dew. For they feed at a time of year when the weather is usually dry, and the moisture within them probably evaporates quickly through their exceptionally thin skins. Experiments show that caterpillars kept in captivity, on leaves artificially sprayed with moisture, do not devour each other but browse together in amity.

The chrysalis (Plate II, 11), which is cunningly disguised as a pointed twig, sleeps head downwards from August to the following May, lashed to a stem by a silken girdle. You will notice that chrysalises (Plate II) thus tied to supports lack the projecting knobs of those that hang by the tail; the excrescences appear to act as buffers, shielding the small, swinging bodies from harm.

Both the Orange-tip and the Bath White belong to the *Pieridae*, a family in which are included also the Large White, *Pieris brassicae* (Plate II, 12) the Small White, *Pieris rapae* (Plate II and 16), the Green-veined White, *Pieris napi* (Plate II), the Wood White, *Leptidea sinapis*, the Black-veined White, *Aporia crataegi* (13, 14), the Brimstone, *Gonepteryx rhamni* (4, 5), the Clouded Yellow, *Colias croceus* (15), and the Pale Clouded Yellow, *Colias hyale*.

8 Peacock Butterflies, *Nymphalis io*, Hibernating

[Smaller than life

9 Peacock Butterflies, *Nymphalis io*, awaking from Hibernation

[Smaller than life

11   Orange-tip, *Eucbloë cardamines*, emerging from Chrysalis   [*Magnification* × 2]

10   Orange-tips, *Eucbloë cardamines*   [*Magnification* × 1½]

The Black-veined White (13, 14) is now, alas, extinct in England, although common enough in France. It was last seen in Kent, and was formerly to be found in Monmouthshire, at Chelsea, then a village, and at Muswell Hill, then green country, now a hideous wilderness of brick and stone. Its loss is to be deplored, for it is of all Whites the most elegant and graceful.

Woodland glades in the south and west of England, and as far north as Cumberland, are the haunt of the uncommon Wood White, whose caterpillar feeds on the vetch. I have never, except in museums, met with this butterfly, but I can't say that I grieve overmuch—its shape is delicate, but it is a flimsy creature, with the texture of tissue paper.

Prettier to my mind, although at times such a pest, are the Common Whites—large (12, and Plate II) and small (16, and Plate II)—both of them residents reinforced by migration—and the Green-veined White, which does not usually migrate. It is innocent of the ravages sometimes attributed to it, for, unlike its cabbage-eating relatives, its caterpillar feeds on the charlock, water-cress, and garlic mustard. You can identify it by the green veins on the yellowish under-surface of its wings. There are, in England, several named forms, and a lovely yellow race, called *Citronea*, occurs in Ireland.

How amazing are the vast migratory journeys of butterflies! We cannot tell what strange longings vex them, what call assembles them, or how their senses respond to the summons; neither do we know the motive that impels them to their wanderings. Is it a search for food or for new breeding-grounds that drives them on? This seems probable, until we reflect that butterflies often fly steadily on through miles of country suitable for breeding-places, and come to rest in barren places where further breeding is impossible. Sometimes the migrants lay eggs on suitable food plants on which they settle for a few minutes during flight; at other times no eggs are laid until the flight is over. Some naturalists think that the migratory urge is a survival from habits acquired long ages ago as a result of climatic, or other conditions; these conditions no longer exist, but deep in the butterfly's nature the instinct remains.

Whatever the reason may be for such extraordinary behaviour, it is certain that these apparently frail insects fly for thousands of miles, both by night and by day, sometimes at a rate of fifteen miles an hour, and often against a head-wind. While on migration they seem possessed by a kind of frenzy, or hysteria. Butterflies of the same species, but from other neighbourhoods, encountered by the migrants on their travels, do not join the wanderers, which fly untiringly, showing uncommon energy and a marked determination to continue in one direction, so that they will fly into the open windows of houses and through railway tunnels sooner than deviate from their set course.

These migratory swarms were mentioned as long ago as 1634 by

Mouffet, who refers to "an army of butterflies, flying like troops in the air, in the year 1104, and they hid the light of the sun like a cloud."

More recent observers also give instances. Charles Darwin, in 1832, noted from his ship, off South America, a vast flock of yellow butterflies. In 1879 a migratory swarm of Painted Ladies appeared in North Africa in April, passed through Barcelona, and reached Minorca by May. They were seen at Sèvres on June 16th, flying north-west; at Angers, 40,000 or more passed up one street in an hour, getting in the way of pedestrians, and as they flew they darkened the day.

Mr. Frohawk quotes the letter of a friend, who relates an experience that befell him as a small boy. While sitting on a cliff near Marazion in Cornwall, he perceived out at sea a yellow patch which, as it came nearer was seen to be a swarm of Clouded Yellows (15) making for the land, flying low over the water and rising and falling over the crest of each wave. The cliffs were soon covered with them, and they stayed in the neighbourhood for several weeks.

In his book, *Out from Brixham*, Colonel Claud Beddington tells how, seeing far off a white cloud which he took for an oncoming squall, he shortened sail, but on nearer approach the cloud resolved itself into an immense swarm of butterflies that settled on the vessel's hull and rigging, like snow.

A French writer, commenting on the appearance in Southern France of swarms of the Large White (12, and Plate II) and the Painted Lady (Frontispiece, Plate I), adds that hunters regard the butterflies as forerunners of quail; if the butterflies are abundant, they hope that the birds will be also.

An instance of several species migrating together was recently observed by Mr. L. Hugh Newman, in Sark. Large and Small Whites appeared first, flying with the east wind, over the sea, from France. Some flew too far out and veered round to regain their direction. With them came Painted Ladies, Clouded Yellows, and Red Admirals. The butterflies alighted for a moment on the thrift growing on the cliffs, then went on their way. The flights continued all day until dusk. Mr. Newman caught some of the butterflies and imprisoned them in a box, and released them after darkness had fallen; whereupon they flew off in the direction taken by the other migrants.

The fact that the Large Cabbage White undertakes mass flights in a definite direction has been known for a hundred and fifty years. There is now, in England, an organisation which watches for the appearance and migration of butterflies; it has obtained the co-operation of the authorities responsible for the lighthouses and lightships round our coast, from which records are also sent in. As a result of these activities and of the observations of various experimental stations, the records of flights have lately increased, and show that the movements of the Large White

13 Mating Pair of Black-veined White Butterflies, *Aporia crataegi*. Female on top

[*About life-size*]

12 Mating Pair of Large White Butterflies, *Pieris brassicae*. Male on top

[*Magnification probably × 1⅛*]

[Magnification × 2]

14 Black-veined White Butterfly, *Aporia cratagi*.
This Butterfly is now extinct in Britain

15 Clouded Yellow Butterfly
Colias croceus

[Magnification × 1½]

group themselves into two main periods, one at the end of May, the second in July, and that the butterflies fly from the Continent towards England, keeping more or less to our coastline, with hardly any return movement in the reverse direction.[1]

Those who have seen Large Whites arriving on our coasts liken them to large snowflakes descending on cliffs and shore.

Companies of Large Whites, Small Whites, Red Admirals and Painted Ladies, these beautiful invaders spread over our countryside; Clouded Yellows and rare Pale Clouded Yellows follow, sometimes in swarms, usually in twos and threes, with a very occasional visit from the rare Long-tailed Blue and the Short-tailed Blue or from the beautiful Queen of Spain Fritillary herself. Two splendid vagrants complete the list—the Camber-well Beauty, an autumn visitor from Scandinavia, and the Monarch, or Milkweed butterfly, which journeys from a far continent to flaunt under our paler skies it great beech-leaf brown, ebony-streaked, pearl-studded wings.

It was formerly supposed that the Monarch, *Danaus plexippus* (17) visited us from its breeding grounds in the Canaries and Cape Verde Islands. Entomological opinion now inclines, however, to the view that the butterfly migrates from America. Milkweed butterflies have been seen half-way across the Atlantic, and they have also been discovered as "stowaways" in potato ships.

The Monarch has another name of Black-veined Brown, to which I prefer its more regal appellation. Apart from its large size and powers of flight, it is interesting as being the only representative in England of the *Danaids*. The males of this foreign family, when making love, hover over the desired one, scattering upon her scented dust. This peculiarity gives them their name, which alludes, of course, to the legend of the imprisoned maiden Danae, whom Zeus visited in a shower of gold.

We are not likely to meet with this grand butterfly as we trundle along our Sussex roads; let us therefore look again at the Whites, with an eye to the beauty of common things.

As we all know, the caterpillars of the Large and Small Whites ravage kitchen gardens, whose exasperated owners perhaps overlook the charm of the ensuing butterflies. These are in both species of two distinct types, the early summer butterflies being pure white in colour, with grey wing-tips, while their offspring, which hatch in August, are larger and more richly creamy, tipped with velvet black. This variation, known as seasonal dimorphism, occurs in other British butterflies, as, for instance, the Comma. In several kinds of foreign butterflies, the difference is

---

[1] New records and information of flights in England or in any other part of the world are still needed, and should be sent to the Keeper of the Entomology Department of the Natural History Museum, London. Such particulars should include the date and locality of the observation, the direction of flight, and either some specimens or a care-ful description of the insects taking part in it. Two or three specimens, no matter how damaged, are of much greater value than a description.

apparent in a much more marked degree. The Large White's second brood produces very handsome insects of which the female is, perhaps, the more striking.

White butterflies are sociable beings and delight in flying in wreaths of five or six or more, like animated pea-blossoms. The colour-sense of these butterflies is well developed, as has recently been proved by Dr. Ilse's experiments with paper "flowers" of different colours. She finds that the Large White, when in search of food, chooses blue and purple colours, and, to a lesser degree, red and yellow: it disregards green, blue-green and grey. But the egg-laying female of this species "drums" with the fore-legs, with which it tests the leaves of the food-plant, and for this reaction it chooses emerald green rather than greenish-blue: yellow and pure blue are neglected. Unlike the bee (which sees red as black and confuses green and yellow) the Large White discriminates between yellow and green and can recognise red. It can also distinguish between bluish-green and grey, colours that are confused by most insects. This is new proof that the system of colour vision in the Cabbage Whites must be different from that of the hive bee and nearer to that of man.[1]

The female Cabbage butterflies (Plate II) will "drum" on any green material—a watering-can, a green dress, green paper—but the "drumming" is difficult to see, as it is performed by regular fore-legs. The "drumming" on paper can be heard a distance of five yards.

The eggs of the Large White are laid in a cluster, those of the Small White singly, on the underside of a cabbage leaf. The microscope reveals them as upright, ribbed vases, golden and translucent, attached to the leaf by their flattened base. Those not eaten by earwigs hatch in about seven days into the caterpillars with which most of us are only too familiar— unattractive even to the fond eye of the most ardent entomologist, those of the Large White (Plate II and 18) are particularly so on account of their gregarious habits and repulsive smell. These creatures have been a pest to mankind since (and probably before) the days of the Greek sage, Aristotle, who watched them eating the cabbages in his garden and found their chrysalises under the eaves of his house. These pests were evidently found throughout the Mediterranean countries in bygone days; for Pliny, the Latin naturalist, tells us that the country people were in the habit of setting up a mare's skull on a stake in the middle of the cabbage patch, as a sort of bogy to frighten away the White butterflies. The survival of this custom could be seen in the last century in the south of France, where an eggshell on a pole was set up in gardens; the idea being that the butterflies, attracted by the whiteness of the eggshell, would lay their eggs on it instead of on the cabbages, and that the young caterpillars would starve to death.

---

[1] The colour vision of butterflies varies in different species. The Small Tortoise-shell is attracted by blue, purple, red and yellow, but neglects green and greenish-yellow.

If cabbages are not available, the caterpillars of the Large and Small Whites will eat wild plants of the same order. All these cruciferous plants contain mustard oil. A Dutch experimenter, Verschaffelt, took a solution of the substance sinigrin, which is present in black mustard, and spread it on leaves of plants of a different order, which the caterpillars had previously refused to eat. Leaves so treated were then devoured, and from these experiments it appears that it is the presence of mustard oil in cruciferous plants that determines their selection as food by the cabbage caterpillars.

Their numbers are to a certain extent kept down by the onslaughts of two or three kinds of parasitic fly. The female of one species lays her eggs in the eggs of the butterfly, and the caterpillars, which hatch with the grubs inside them, are doomed from the first. Another fly is always on the look-out for a likely caterpillar, in whose back she inserts her ovipositor once, twice, thrice and again, laying an egg each time. The grubs suck the juices of the caterpillar without interfering with its vital organs, and the damage is at first not apparent. But the unfortunate victim dwindles, and, near the time of its pupating, dies, and the full-fed maggots (18) crawl out of the body of their expiring host, and spin, on or near its shrivelled carcase, their small yellow cocoons (19) from which, in due course, appear more of these horrid flies.

The chrysalises of the Large and Small Whites (Plate II), attached by a silken girdle, are hidden in corners, or behind a ledge, or window-sill, usually in an outhouse or potting-shed. The offspring of August butterflies begin their pupal sleep about mid-September and hatch the following spring, when their numbers are sometimes reinforced by the migratory hosts already mentioned. The number of migrants varies from year to year; during one summer thousands arrive, while in the next, a few only are to be seen.

Two yellow members of this family, the Clouded Yellow (15) and the Pale Clouded Yellow, belong to the group on account of morphological similarities. Like other Whites, they use all their six legs in walking, and the neuration of their wings is similar. Butterflies are largely classified according to variations of these two characteristics, which enable us also to recognise the kinship of English butterflies with those found abroad.

The Clouded Yellow, *Colias croceus* is an exciting butterfly—vivid, a fast flier. Catching a glimpse of it from our caravan window, we cast aside spoons and saucepans, leaving the dinner to burn, and rush out in pursuit of the saffron shape disappearing over the brow of the hill. We are fortunate in discovering it clinging to a clover-head in an adjacent field where stands a notice-board marked TRESPASSERS WILL BE PROSECUTED—and, also a bull. Regardless, in our entomological zeal, of the law and of our personal safety, we creep cautiously nearer, feasting our eyes on the golden one . . . do not capture him! Like us, he is enjoying life; he will find a mate, and their five hundred caterpillar progeny, will, we hope, escape the enemies that lie in wait for them, to produce in September a second brood of butterflies. I will give you a Clouded Yellow from my own collection, and then, when fog looms and green fields are far away, you can gaze your fill on the glowing yellow and orange and the greenish undertones of those dark-tipped wings.

16 Small Whites, *Pieris rapae*

17 The Monarch, *Danaus plexippus*. An occasional migrant from North America

[*Slightly larger than life*

PLATE III.

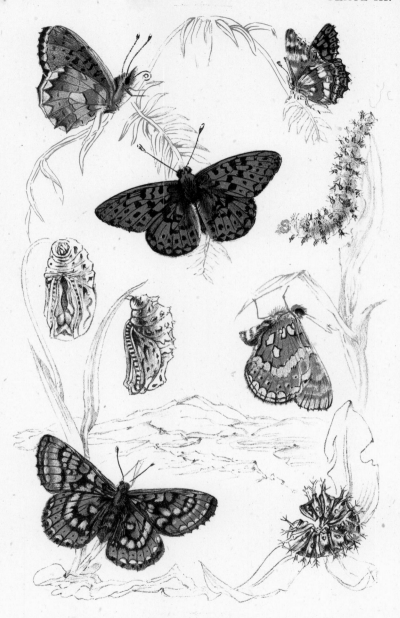

Top left: PEARL BORDERED FRITILLARY, UNDERSIDE.   *Top right:* DUKE OF BURGUNDY FRITILLARY.   *Top centre:* PEARL BORDERED FRITILLARY, MALE. *Middle right:* CATERPILLAR OF ISLE OF WIGHT FRITILLARY.   *Middle left:* CHRYSALISES OF MARSH FRITILLARY.   *Lower left:* MARSH FRITILLARY.   *Lower right:* MARSH FRITILLARY, UNDERSIDE. *Bottom right:* CATERPILLAR OF MARSH FRITILLARY.

CHAPTER IV

The Forest

As we approach the New Forest, the countryside changes. The chalk downs of Sussex end in a great bluff, Hampshire fields and hedgerows become less cared for, and beech woods merge into oak glades and common land over which birches wave their delicate plumes. And here, among the glades and thickets, the bog and heather of this ancient place, are to be found a variety of butterflies.

Eminent among these—most subtly beautiful, I think, of all our butterflies—are the Fritillaries. Gold and silver, magically wrought and studded with crystalline jewels, contrast with jade and blackest jet in the mosaic of their wings. Poetry is in their names, Aglaia, Euphrosyne, Selene; and as we delightedly watch them, and think of the legends which these names evoke, it seems that the Moon-goddess indeed descends again to earth, in the quiet of these primæval places.

We must wait for July for the splendid High-brown, the Dark Green and the Silver-washed fritillaries, about which there is more to be written later. May brings the Pearl-bordered and the Small Pearl-bordered, *Argynnis euphrosyne* and *Argynnis selene*, frail creatures that droop like enamelled pendants from twigs, or flutter among moss and violets, by secret streams and in the glades of the forest. The Pearl-bordered Fritillary (Plate III), once known as the April butterfly, differs from her companion in her lighter colour and markings; she has nine pearls on her underside, whereas *Selene* (Plate VI) has about twenty. Both lay their eggs in May on the dog-violet, and the ensuing spiny caterpillar has an odd life-cycle, for instead of eating its fill while violet leaves are plentiful, it prefers to creep away, when quite small, to the dead leaves and twigs at the root of its plant, where it spins a little web; and here it hibernates until the following March, when it emerges to feed again, and to spend a short time suspended as a hump-backed chrysalis.

Damp places are usually the haunt of the Marsh fritillary, *Euphydryas aurinia* (Plate III), formerly known as the Greasy Fritillary, which can be recognised by the chequering of its wedge-shaped wings and by their slightly glossy or greasy surface. This Fritillary does not occupy quite such a warm place in my affections as the April butterfly, perhaps on account of its less idyllic associations. It is restricted in range, though not rare; I have found it in Wiltshire, in early June, and it occurs among other places on Hod Hill, in Dorset. It is the most locally variable of all the Fritillaries. The form found in Kent is small, with a background of brick red and no cream-coloured markings. The Irish form is larger and much more distinctly chequered, with marked patches of cream.

Butterflies found in the West Country are different again. Their gregarious caterpillars spin on their food-plant, the devil's-bit scabious, a bag-like web, in which they all huddle during the winter, coming out on warm days to sun themselves. When half-grown they disperse and feed singly until their pupating. A naturalist has seen a cuckoo feeding on one of these "nests".

A plague of these caterpillars (Plate III), occurred in 1884 in Shropshire, where a clergyman observed numbers of them crawling everywhere. Another clergyman (they seem to be observant people) in Ireland[1] drove out to see a reported "shower of worms" and found fields and roads blackened by fritillary larvæ in writhing masses. That the swarm was short of food was evident, for the resulting butterflies were very small and pale.

A still more extraordinary instance occurred about fifteen years ago, also in Ireland, in Co. Fermanagh, where the caterpillars swarmed in such masses that the farmers gathered them up with forks and stacked them in heaps and burnt them in great bonfires.

The Heath Fritillary, *Melitaea athalia* (21), is local in June in woods in the east and south of England. Its caterpillar feeds on the cow-wheat, which spreads in clearings when a wood is cut. The caterpillar therefore follows the wood-cutter, and the haunts of the butterfly change from year to year. Its under-surface has a distinctive pattern, bold and regular, like the white keys of a piano. The caterpillars hibernate throughout the winter, three or four together in a rolled-up leaf.

We shall not meet with the Isle of Wight Fritillary, *Melitaea cinxia* (20), on this trip, for it is to be found only on sudden slopes and cliffs in the Isle of Wight, where the caterpillars (Plate III), feed in a web on the spear-leaved plantain. They separate during the end of April and crawl away to pupate, and the butterfly emerges in June. It has an under-surface marked with wavy lines, like lace, or embroidery.

You would never think, to look at him, that a small personage with a consequential title, the Duke of Burgundy Fritillary (*Hamearis lucina*) (Plate III), would claim the name of the larger Fritillaries, for in appearance he resembles those dumpy butterflies, the Skippers. His chequered markings seem to be his only excuse for pushing behaviour, for classification places him in solitary state, the only English member of a family characteristic of Tropical regions, the *Erycinidae*.

This very local insect flies in May and June, in the clearings and glades of woods in the south of England. The caterpillar feeds on the cowslip and primrose, and the hairy pupa rests for over eight months, attached to withered leaves by a tail-pad and girdle of silk.

We must now leave the forest; but as we bump over the grass of our camping-ground on our way to the open road, we pass through a grove of ancient holly-trees, whose trunks gleam like marble beneath their dark

[1] Recorded by Mr. Kane in his Lepidoptera of Ireland.

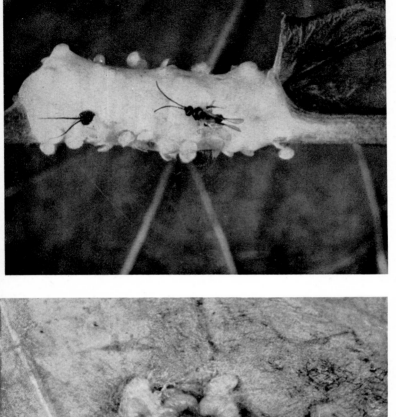

18 Ichneumon Grubs crawling out of Large White's, *Pieris brassicae*, Caterpillar

[*Magnification* × 2]

19 Ichneumon Fly crawling out of a group of Cocoons on Large White's, *Pieris brassicae*, Chrysalis

[*Magnification* × 2]

21 Heath Fritillary, *Melitaea athalia*, on Bugle

[*Magnification* × 1¾]

20 Isle of Wight Fritillary, *Melitaea cinxia*
(underside)

[*Magnification* × 1½]

leaves. A small lavender-blue butterfly claims our attention here—a Holly Blue, *Celastrina argiolus* (Plate IV), the only woodland member of a family that, as a rule, loves the open downs. The female lays her eggs on the young leaves of the holly, where the green caterpillars feed at night. They produce, in July and August, a second brood of butterflies, that now lay their eggs on the tiny unopened buds of the ivy; the young caterpillars eat their way into the buds and are difficult to find unless one cuts these open. They are full-fed in five or six weeks' time and pass the winter as chrysalises attached by a silken girdle to the underside of an ivy leaf. Females of this second brood are sometimes marked by darker wing-tips and by a smudge of black across the fore pair.

This engaging butterfly used to be known as the Blue-speckt, or Azure Blue. You can identify it by its silver-grey, black-speckled under-surface, that lacks the orange spots of the other commoner Blues. You will meet it in gardens and lanes, as well as in woods. It has a habit, noticeable in other Blues, of sleeping a good deal in the daytime, especially on dull days, when you may come across it, ensconced on a leaf amid some little bower of greenery, where it appears rather conspicuous from its silvery colour. Its slumbers are deep, and you can peer closely at its black-and-white-ringed antennæ, its fluffy white face and black eyes. But you will need a microscope to perceive the odd trait that it shares with the other Blues—namely, that these eyes are hairy.

CHAPTER V
The Fens

It is a far cry from the glades of the New Forest to the fens of East Anglia. For naturalists of the eighteenth century such a journey would have been a considerable undertaking, involving a long ride, by coach or on horseback, halts at inns to sleep and to change horses, with the probability of getting stuck in the mud or of being attacked by highwaymen. But though these were uncomfortable days, they were fruitful and exciting also to entomologists, who beheld, on lonely heaths, or among the then undrained fens, or in green fields now covered with houses, many butterflies now extinct in England, or exceedingly rare; the Mazarine Blue, the Large Blue, the Black-veined White, the Purple Emperor, the Large Copper, and the superb creature that we have come to-day to seek: the Swallow-tail.

It is a melancholy thought that a butterfly plentiful, not so long ago, in "the Battersea and Tottenham marshes near London" and throughout the fens of Suffolk, Cambridgeshire and Lincolnshire, should have been driven from many of its haunts by the encroaches of towns and the draining and reclaiming of fen land. The Swallow-tail is, however, still common on the Norfolk Broads and in Wicken Fen, and it is being re-established in new localities with the aid of landowners and of the B.B.C. The Swallow-tail's haunts are now guarded, not by a many-headed Hydra, but by a polite Fen Watcher who asks for your permit (obtainable from the authorities of the National Trust) and who sees to it that you capture one or two butterflies only.

Wicken Fen's chief feature is its flatness. The ground is tufted with sallow-bushes and tangled with the plants of the marsh—brooklime, forget-me-not, fennel, marsh dropwort—through which we push our way. Look! There it is, our butterfly, incongruously perched on an umbel of parsley—its tiger-striped, swallow-tailed wings outspread to display their ruby eyes; an improbable-looking creature, which would more fitly be enthroned on a cactus flower or a scarlet Pointsettia; *Papilio machaon*, the only English member of a family that comprises some of the largest and most beautiful butterflies in the world. No wonder that, with these exotic relations, the Swallow-tail should seem something of a foreigner itself—a beautiful alien, astray in a northern fen.

I do not know why, in England, it prefers to live in a fen on the cold East Coast, unless it be that it retains the home chosen in ages past, when East Anglia formed part of low-lying lands joined to the Continent, up whose valleys it would doubtless make its way from the warm countries of the south. In France you will find it among olive-trees and vineyards,

22 Swallowtail, *Papilio machaon*, just emerged

[*Magnification about* × 1¼

23   Green Hairstreak, *Callophrys rubi*

[*Magnification* × 2

24   Brown Hairstreak, *Thecla betulae*

[*Magnification* × 2

on the grilling hillsides of the Midi, where the caterpillar must of necessity feed on plants that grow in an arid soil; and, too, in the meadows of Normandy and on the high pastures of the mountains.

In England the Swallow-tail, *Papilio machaon* (22), has two broods. Eggs laid in May or June hatch in about ten days into handsome, yellow-green, black-ringed caterpillars, which feed on the Wild Carrot, *Daucus carota*, and the Milk Parsley, *Peucedanum palustre*. When danger threatens they put out two little horns, like those of a snail, and emit an evil smell. They become full-fed about July. Some of their chrysalises do not emerge until the following May, whilst others hatch in August, to breed again that year. Both generations are found in winter in reed beds, attached to a dead reed by a silken girdle.[1]

Female Swallow-tails kept in captivity will "drum" on green material, but they will lay eggs only on objects which have the same form and consistency as their natural food-plant, the wild carrot. One captive female, observed by Dora Ilse, laid a number of eggs on a dried fern.

The why and wherefore of our Papilio's second name must remain one of the puzzles of nomenclature. Machaon was, as you may remember, one of the two medical officers who accompanied the Greek army to Troy. He may have been interested in butterflies, though I cannot remember anything to that effect in the story. His brother, Podalirius the surgeon, has bequeathed his name to *Papilio podalirius*, the scarce Swallow-tail, a splendid butterfly which has been known to migrate to England, on rare occasions, from the Continent.

And now we must take the road again. We wander westward, through Suffolk by-roads, past farmlands, carefully tended, and fields of young wheat, in a countryside all glorious with white and gold; gold of the buttercup fields, white of heavy-scented hawthorn and of the stitchwort that fills the hedges with drifts of frosted crystal. We stop at the edge of a little wood that slopes down to the road, and pick bluebells, and yellow archangel. The wood leads to a common, and here, among Orange-tips and Whites, a small green butterfly suddenly appears and disappears—a Green Hairstreak, *Callophrys rubi* (23), adept at this vanishing trick, for its brown wings have a grass-green underside, and when, alighting, it closes them, it melts at once into the background of foliage. The single-brooded caterpillars feed on the dogwood, the broom, and the bird's foot lotus, *Lotus corniculatus*, and also on each other; but a long sleep keeps them out of further mischief, for their chrysalis state endures from July until the following May.

There are other Hairstreaks, neat little woodland butterflies, that we shall see in July. They are allied to the Blues and are classified in the same

[1] For an account of the rare black form of the Swallow-tail, sometimes found on the Norfolk Broads, I refer my readers to Mr. L. Hugh Newman's book *Wings in the Sun*, published by E. J. Arnold & Son, price 1*s*.

family, the *Lycaenidae*, of which the female members possess six walking legs, while the males use four only, the front pair being rudimentary.

Let us now hurry on to the Wiltshire downs. The last days of May have slipped away, and discoveries await us with the new month. In the fens, we have seen one of the largest of British butterflies; on the downs, we shall see some of the smallest.

PLATE IV.

1. HOLLY BLUE, MALE. 1a. HOLLY BLUE MALE, UNDERSIDE. 1b. HOLLY
BLUE FEMALE. 2. COMMON BLUE, MALE. 2a. COMMON BLUE, FEMALE.
2b. PAIR OF COMMON BLUES. 3. SILVER-STUDDED BLUE, UNDERSIDE. 4.
ADONIS BLUE, MALE. 4a. ADONIS BLUE, FEMALE. 4b. ADONIS BLUE
FEMALE, UNDERSIDE. 4c. ADONIS BLUE MALE, UNDERSIDE. 5. CHALK-
HILL BLUE, MALE. 5a. CHALKHILL BLUE, FEMALE. 5b. PAIR OF CHALK-
HILL BLUES. 6. BROWN ARGUS BLUE. 6a. BROWN ARGUS BLUE, UNDER-
SIDE. 7. LITTLE BLUE. 7a. LITTLE BLUE, UNDERSIDE.

CHAPTER VI

The Downs

WE will camp on Salisbury Plain, in a coomb of the chalk downs that are so curiously piled and folded by the sea that once covered them. An escarpment shelters us from the wind that here blows always—a wind sometimes keen and cruel, now tempered to a gentle breeze coming in little puffs. Around us, the sheep-cropped turf is matted with tiny, sweet-smelling flowers—purple thyme, yellow rockrose, blue and white milkwort, pink restharrow, yellow trefoil, white clover, yellow balls of medick and reddish knobs of burnet. This garden provides green food and nectar for its colony of inhabitants, and it is the playground also of these diminutive people—snails, flies, beetles, moths, caterpillars and their resulting butterflies—Skippers and Small Heaths, and large companies of Blues.

Among the smaller butterflies the Blues are my favourites. Everything about them endears them to me; their heavenly colour; their willingness to stay still to be looked at when clustered two or three together on a scabious head; their association with the tiny exquisite downland plants; the curious egg that the mother places so fastidiously, one on each plant.

Three blue butterflies in particular appeal to me; those named Icarus, Bellargus and Coridon. These seem to embody the very spirit of the downs. It is as if wind and rain, sunshine and cloud, had poured their essence into some magic crucible, there to be transmuted into the colours of butterflies' wings—blue colours that have in them something of fire and ice, with the sheen of grass that is stroked by the wind, and the depth of the sky reflected in water.

Polyommatus icarus, the Common Blue (Plate IV and 25), is to be found in open spaces all over England, but chiefly on the chalk. We see its May brood around us here. The second brood will fly in August and September. Only the male glories in wings of blue. Those of the female are smoky-brown, usually dusted with blue, with a border of orange dots on their upper surface. Below, both sexes are similarly speckled.

There is an Irish form of this butterfly in which the female is almost as blue as the male, with a chain of bright orange spots on the upper surface of the wings. Among sandhills on the west coast of Ireland a certain proportion of gynandromorph[1] butterflies occur: their wings are those of a male on one side, those of a female on the other. There are several aberrations to be found in England also. In one of them, the black dots on the under-surface are enlarged into streaks, like splashes of Indian ink.

[1] These gynandrous butterflies are commonly intersexes, *not* hermaphrodites, the latter being creatures in which both sexes are functionally present.

Bird's-foot lotus,[1] black medick and restharrow are the food plants of the caterpillar, which resembles a green woodlouse. Those that are the offspring of August butterflies hibernate from September to the following May, when they feed up and spend a short time lashed to a leaf as a squat green chrysalis.

On cold, cloudy days these butterflies cluster on grass-stems with their wings tightly shut and sleep away the hours till the sun shines. Seen thus, with only their greyish-speckled undersides showing, they look like triangular scraps of paper blown into the grass by the wind. Shake the grass, and up fly the butterflies; the air is full of shining fragments of blue that dance up and down like motes in a sunbeam. Then down they all drop deep into the grass, and sink once more into a profound slumber.

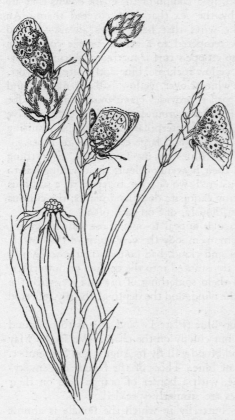

In company with the Common Blue we see the Brown Argus Blue, *Aricia agestis* (Plate IV), a brown little creature, with no trace of blue but with orange marginal dots above and below in both sexes. Rather a dull butterfly—I tolerate it out of politeness to its relations. Its dumpy caterpillar, which hibernates, feeds on the rockrose and stork's-bill. The second brood flies in August and September.

I have never found the less common Silver-studded Blue, *Plebejus argus* (Plate IV), on the chalk downs, but I have seen it in Suffolk. It usually frequents sandy heaths and commons. You can recognise it by the silver spots on its underwings and by the shape of its wings, which are more rounded than those of the Common Blue, and of a more purple blue. The caterpillar feeds on the flowers of the gorse and broom.

Top left: Chalk-hill Blue, *Lysandra coridon*
Middle and right: Common Blue,
Polyommatus icarus, asleep among grasses
(*Life-size*)

You cannot mistake the midget Small Blue, *Cupido minimus* (Plate IV),

[1] *Lotus corniculatus.*

25　Common Blue (female), *Polyommatus icarus*

[*Magnification* × 2

26　Male Adonis Blue, *Lysandra bellargus*

[*Magnification* × 2¼

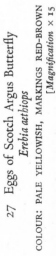

27 Eggs of Scotch Argus Butterfly
Erebia aethiops

COLOUR: PALE YELLOWISH, MARKINGS RED-BROWN
[*Magnification* × 15]

28 Eggs of Speckled Wood Butterfly, *Pararge aegeria*

COLOUR: WHITE, WITH GREENISH TINGE

[*Magnification* × 15]

it is so very diminutive; and, besides, it is extremely local—a solitary little being—and it has no orange dots on its under-surface. It is partially double-brooded and spends ten months as a caterpillar, hibernating and awaking to feed on the kidney vetch.

Lovelier far than these is the Adonis Blue, *Lysandra bellargus* (Plate IV and 26), a creature vivid as a humming-bird. If you do not know its haunts you may walk for miles in vain, for it is widely distributed on chalk downs in the south of England. But if you are fortunate, you may come upon a stretch of turf flashing with the blue of this living jewel. Unlike the Common Blue (Plate IV), and the Brown Argus (Plate IV), which congregate among knapweed and in the tall grass of lynchets and hollows, Adonis prefers the short turf. Here it flickers to and fro and here the mother butterfly lays her beautiful eggs, one on each plant of the horse-shoe vetch. The first brood of caterpillars feed in April and early May and are on the wing in June and the second hatch in September, to hibernate until the following May.

The azure wings of Adonis are delicately fringed with alternate black and white checks (Plate IV and 26), and their underside is richer in colour and more copiously spotted than that of the slightly smaller Icarus. Like the Common Blue and the Chalk-hill Blue (Plate IV), the female Adonis retains, for protection, the brownish garb once prevalent among all her kind. For scientists tell us that when butterflies first appeared on this earth, they were coloured only with brown, black and white, brown preponderating among the females, who were thus rendered inconspicuous whilst about their important business of egg-laying. During the course of ages, white changed to yellow, and then to orange and red; black became modified to purple and blue and other colours gradually appeared, while as a means to the end of reproducing the species, the male acquired brilliant tints wherewith to please the female and to excite her to yield to his advances.

Downland slopes favoured by Adonis support, in late July and early August and during September, one brood of a rival beauty, *Lysandra coridon*, the Chalk-hill Blue (Plate IV). A black border fringed with white enhances the sheen of its wings, that are neither moonlight blue, nor green, nor silver, but a suggestion of all three. To see them coldly gleaming near the cerulean of adonis, amid a maze of harebells and of purple campanula, is a vision never to be forgotten.

Equally memorable is the sight of cow-dung constellated by this butterfly, to which the juices of animal droppings are, particularly in dry weather, as alluring as the sweetest flower.

Coridon is a much commoner butterfly than Adonis. You will find colonies of these butterflies all over the downs, on close-cropped turf and among the rough grass of banks. The caterpillar feeds on the horseshoe vetch, on which the egg, laid in August, lies dormant through the winter to hatch in the following May.

Fitting cradles for the butterfly's perfection are the eggs of Adonis and

Coridon—curiously beautiful objects, in shape like lidded bowls, their surface encrusted with a reticulated pattern. Of the two, the egg of Adonis is the more delicately wrought.

There is something very touching in the care lavished by Nature on the decoration of these tiny eggs, which probably has a protective purpose; for the flutings and chisellings that adorn their surface, though invisible to our unaided vision, may be apparent to the sight of birds and predatory insects, which are deluded into taking them for galls or excrescences of the leaf, the pores and veinings of which they so cunningly simulate. Each family has its own casket. The Peacock, the Red Admiral, the Tortoiseshell and their kin produce urns, the curves of which are accentuated by symmetrically spaced ribs that converge at the apex. In the Large Tortoiseshell, these ribs are enlarged into delicate keels, rather like the fins of a fish. Ribbing adorns the dome-like egg of the Skipper; the Fritillary's is like a squat tub; the Small Heath has a green basket with a sunken lid; the Brimstone makes a tall fluted vase; while the egg of the White-letter Hairstreak is unique, an extraordinary spiny affair, like a pincushion stuck full of pins.

We must now return to our caravan, for the wind comes in gusts, and in the sky appear the signs and portents of rain. Let us pack up and speed on to the more sheltered woods and vales of Dorset. We have seen all the commoner Blues: four remain. Of these, the Mazarine Blue became extinct sixty years ago and more, while the Long-tailed Blue and the Short-tailed Blue are rare migrants. The former, which is a Mediterranean species, has been captured about eighteen times in this country. An instance of its breeding in Great Britain was observed by Mr. L. Hugh Newman, who tells me that while reading in the garden during a holiday in Sark, he suddenly became aware that an unfamiliar butterfly had flown by. He saw it settle on a lupin and recognised it by its spots and tails as a Long-tailed Blue, *Lampides boeticus*. He caught the butterfly and imprisoned her in a muslin bag which he tied round the lupin, in the centre of whose flowers she proceeded to lay her eggs. As the flowers faded, the eggs adhered to the growing pods; in a fortnight these assumed a peppered appearance, and the slug-like caterpillars were found inside. When full-fed they turned in a night from green to purple and lashed themselves to the pods where they remained ten days as chrysalises. The emerging butterflies, which had a lovely, grape-like bloom, were all bought by Lord Rothschild, whose collection of butterflies can be seen in the Museum at Tring.

The Short-tailed Blue, *Everes argiades*, has been recorded six times only in the last fifty years and was seen in Sussex in 1931.

The Large Blue, *Maculinea arion*, is the largest, and now the rarest of our resident blue butterflies, If you are lucky enough to discover it, you cannot mistake its wings of twilight blue, shot with bronze and blotched with black. For years nothing was known of its life-history, until in 1902, or thereabouts, Mr. Frohawk watched, and recorded, the extraordinary proceedings which I will summarise as follows:

The female butterfly lays her eggs in late June or early July, on a plant of thyme that grows over an ant's nest, and the young caterpillar at first so much resembles the thyme blossoms on which it feeds as to be practically invisible. In early life it has cannibalistic habits which cease about the time of its third moult, when its appearance becomes excessively odd. It now has a tiny head, a long neck and a body distended and shiny; on its back appears a honey-gland, which secretes drops of a sweet liquid. The ants, which up to the present have taken no notice of the caterpillar, now evince the greatest interest in it, smelling and licking it, and stroking it with their antennæ. To these advances the caterpillar responds by secreting more honey, which the ants eagerly imbibe.

After its third moult the caterpillar rests for a few days and then begins to wander about till it meets an ant, which shows signs of great excitement, walking round and round the caterpillar and "milking" it. This goes on for an hour or more. The caterpillar then signals that it is ready to be carried off. It swells its front half and hunches up its back like an angry cat; the ant gets astride of it, seizes it behind the "hunch" and sets off for the nest. Upon arrival, it is saluted by the other ants, who make way for it, and it descends with his burden into the inner chambers. Here the caterpillar is tended by the ants, who feed it upon their larvæ, on which diet it becomes white and fat and three times its former size. In return for board and lodging it exudes a sweet liquid for the benefit of its hosts. At the approach of winter it settles down for hibernation in a deep cavity where ant larvæ in their last stages are tended by the workers. In the spring it awakens and without moving begins to feed again. It goes on eating, in the dark, until June, when it arrives at full growth without having moulted since the previous August. When ready to pupate, it attaches itself to the roof of its chamber where it remains suspended, then drops, to lie for another twenty-one days. At the end of this time the butterfly emerges, and, still soft and crumpled, makes its way through the tortuous passages of the nest and out at the front door, there to dry its wings in the sunshine.

After this adventurous year of preparation the perfect insect lives only for a few weeks.

When this life-history became known collectors flocked to the butterfly's haunts in Cornwall and dug up all the ants' nests they could find in order to breed specimens for their collections, with the result that the butterfly has now become exceedingly rare. Several localities are now carefully preserved as breeding-grounds and I can assure you that in the right season it is now possible to see these butterflies in reasonable numbers "somewhere in the west country".

It is, I believe, still extant in other places and I once saw a solitary specimen in Wiltshire; which gives me hope that these blue wings await me, one day, somewhere on the downs that I love.

5

CHAPTER VII

Hedgerow and Hillside

OUR engine gives a groan and expires; our utmost efforts fail to resuscitate her. There is nothing for it but to tramp the seven miles to Blandford, there to implore help from the garage.

As we trudge through the rain, our footsteps disturb one after another of that common butterfly, the Meadow Brown, *Maniola jurtina* (Plate V), that flutters a few yards to subside again into the drenched grass. On such a wet walk I became embittered towards this ubiquitous creature, although kinder feelings eventually prevailed; for then I read that the male Meadow Brown bears on his wings a tuft of hairs connecting with scent-producing scales[1] that emit their perfume when the hairs are raised and opened fanwise, and that he uses this scent as an enticement to his bride. And I was glad to think that the poor dowdy creature was thus compensated for the lack of the brilliant colours that adorn other butterflies; and that he possessed a faculty that distinguishes those much grander butterflies, the foreign Danaids. And then I observed the Meadow Brown's egg, which is like the neatest of woven baskets—and finally, by a happy chance, I came to see the charm of the Meadow Brown.

It was on a shining evening after rain that I beheld in a meadow an array of thistles, upstanding like a screen of wrought steel. And on their purple tassels, and among the great white trumpets of convolvulus tangled in the grass below, there fluttered and alighted a host of brown butterflies, so that the gaunt stems seemed to blossom with wings. The slanting sun showed the veined pattern of their upper surface, and the earth-colours of their underwings. No two were alike; one female appeared mouse-brown, another tawny, while the light patches that mark her wings varied from sandy to leaf-brown. Of the males, some were umber in hue, others almost black, and a few bore patches of smoky white.[2] Their languid flight had not the Fritillary's grace, yet they too praised life. I watched the brown butterflies till the sun cooled and they dropped down, one by one, into the grass to sleep; only the thistles remained, austere and vigilant, against the evening sky.

Let us employ the pause occasioned by our breakdown by looking at the Meadow Brown's allies, the *Satyridae*, most of which are common in the hedgerows round our stranded caravan. Like the Fauns and Satyrs, whose namesakes they are, they are creatures of the field and woodland, seldom to be met with in gardens. All begin life as fork-tailed caterpillars coloured green or brown to resemble the grass on which they feed at

---

[1] These are apparent as a disc, or brand, near the centre of the upper wing.
[2] This is a form of albinism, due to lack of pigment in the scales of the wing.

PLATE V.

Top left: WALL BUTTERFLY, UNDERSIDE.　　*Top right:* HEDGE BROWN.　*Top centre:* SPECKLED WOOD, UNDERSIDE.　　*Middle left:* SPECKLED WOOD. *Middle right:* RINGLET.　　*Lower centre:* MEADOW BROWN, FEMALE.　　*Lower left:* WALL BUTTERFLY.　　*Lower right:* GRAYLING, UNDERSIDE, WITH RINGLET CATERPILLAR, JUST ABOVE.

night, and further disguised by stripes that simulate the mid-rib of the blade.

Almost as common as the Meadow Brown is the Hedge Brown (Plate V), or Gatekeeper, *Maniola tithonus*, whose smaller russet-brown wings with their tawny patches and one black spot on the underside are familiar among the bramble and hazel of every summer hedgerow. It differs from the continuously brooded Meadow Brown in that it produces one numerous brood in June and July. The caterpillar hibernates through the winter.

The Small Heath, *Coenonympha pamphilus*, is a neat little fawn-coloured butterfly which flies over downland and open heaths in company with Burnet moths and Common Blues. On windy days you will find it clinging to a knapweed head, with its wings shut, concealing their one black eye.

Its north-country cousin, the Large Heath, *Coenonympha tullia*, first discovered near the town which gave it its former name of Manchester Argus, frequents swampy moorlands, where are to be found many local races of the butterfly.

You must go north also to see two allied butterflies, the Scotch Argus, *Erebia aethiops*, and the Small Mountain Ringlet, *Erebia epiphron*, but as our mishap precludes a visit thither, let us fly in fancy till we alight on some bleak, but romantic, fell in Cumberland or Westmorland, or, if you will, on a Scotch mountain wreathed in mist, where, among bilberries and heather, our two butterflies endeavour to warm themselves in the pale sunshine of this chilly land. You will see that the dark chocolate-coloured wings of the Scotch Argus are banded with red that shows up a row of black eyes; while the ringlets of the smaller butterfly are apparent both on the upper and the underside of his dark brown wings.

Here in Dorset the rain is over. The clouds trail away like a curtain that is lifted, and all the green things give thanks. Spicy odours ascend from the refreshed earth, and beetles and butterflies and small winged flies creep and flutter towards the sun. The bramble-blossom is heavy with the feasting throng—Meadow Brown (Plate V), Hedge Brown (Plate V), Speckled Wood, *Pararge aegeria* (Plate V and 28), and Ringlet, *Aphantopus hyperantus* (Plate V and 30), a languid creature which aspires only to the lowest spray. Its dark glossy wings have a nap that tarnishes all too quickly. Their olive under-surface is distinctly ringed with white-circled black dots, larger in the female. These ringed spots are apt to vary among butterflies of different localities. Sometimes they are well marked, sometimes they disappear entirely. In one variety, *Arete*, the rings are absent but the white dots are apparent. In another, *Obsoleta*, neither rings nor spots are to be seen. *Caeca* has white dots on the hind wings, but the front wings are plain. *Lanceolata* has large, pear-shaped spots, conspicuously ringed.

The Ringlet (Plate V and 30) is a thoughtful mother, and hides her eggs by dropping them into the grass—and as they are rounded, like miniature ping-pong balls with dents in them, they roll down among the roots, where the small caterpillars hibernate from August to the following spring.

The Ringlet is pretty, in an inanimate way, but livelier and more appealing is the Speckled Wood, *Pararge aegeria* (Plate V), which charms us immediately by its creamy-dappled dusky colouring and graceful flight, and by its pretty way of pirouetting to display the buff and brown pencillings and spots and the wavy lines of the underwings. The down on the butterfly's back has green glints, which give a finishing touch to its elegance. It emerges from the chrysalis in early April and delights us until May, and in July and August second and third broods appear and remain with us up to the last days of September and even into October. The pretty creatures love the half-light of leafy lanes, where their dappled wings are one with the shadows. Couch-grass, cocksfoot and annual meadow grass provide food for the green caterpillars which emerge from hibernation to feed during the winter if the weather is mild.

To see the Marbled White, *Melanargia galathea*, which is not a White at all, but a member of this same Satyr family—we must retrace our steps to the downland, where, in sheltered hollows here and there, the tall sheep's fescue grass supports colonies of this lovely and local butterfly, which it is always a joy to discover. It never strays far from home, where it flutters to and fro over the grasses with the lazy flight peculiar to its kind. I should like it to be called by its old name of "The Marmoris" or "Our Half-mourner". Its German title of "Backgammon-board" is apt, though it hardly describes the loveliness of the wings, that have the colour of new milk before the cream has risen, while their black chequerings are softer than velvet. The "Marmoress" drops her eggs into the grass, where the young caterpillar hatches in August. After eating its eggshell, it hibernates without further sustenance until December. It then awakes and feeds continuously until the June following its August birthday. When full-fed it attaches itself to a grass-blade where it hangs for about ten days only as a chrysalis. The emerging butterflies crawl up grass-stems to dry their wings, whose exquisite, mealy underside you can admire at leisure, for they are in no hurry to be off on their initial flight.

No holiday is complete without a sight of the sea; and as our caravan is now ready to take the road again, we will travel south to the coast of the Isle of Purbeck, where we can see the two remaining Satyrs, the Wall Butterfly, *Pararge megera* (Plate V), and the Grayling, *Eumenis semele* (Plate V), both of which are common on the heathery lands round Wareham and among the hills that drop down to the coves and tangled cliffs of this beautiful corner of Britain.

It is pleasant to lie on the hillside on this June day, and to listen to the voices of the wind. Gusty voices rush through the air, secret voices whisper in the grasses that bend and rise again in the breeze like bristling fur beneath the caress of an invisible hand. And with the voice of the wind comes the fitful murmur of the sea.

I listen, and I think of the pageant of the ages, and of the winged lizards and monsters that dwelt on those shores in prehistoric times. Their fossilised remains are still to be found dug from rock and clay. And I remember that in one such rock-bed, dating from the tertiary period, there has been found the imprint of a butterfly's wing.

No monstrous shapes disturb our peace to-day, but the Wall Butterfly basks on the rock as doubtless its ancestors did three million years before man appeared on earth. It loves drought and heat, and you will find it (in June and again in August) in open places where there are rocks or stone walls on which it suns itself and amidst whose grey and gold lichens it mimics. Sometimes in dry upland pastures it seeks the honey of scabious and knapweed in company with Blues and Meadow Browns. Its

Marbled White, *Melanargia galathea*
(*Rather less than life-size*)

black and tawny chequering might cause it to be mistaken for a Fritillary, but a second glance shows that it lacks the distinction and the rapid flight of these peerless butterflies.

The single-brooded Grayling—formerly called the Rock-eyed Underwing—is remarkable for its protective colouring. It never settles with open wings as do other butterflies and I have seldom observed it to alight on a flower,[1] except, now and then, the bramble, or to feed at all during the four or five weeks of its life. For security it prefers to rest with wings closed on dry earth or rock, or among the charred debris left by a heath fire, where its extraordinary resemblance to its chosen background renders it almost invisible—it is surprising to see a pointed stone take wing and fly away.

Butterflies seem to possess some sense that guides them to protective backgrounds. It is interesting to watch this choice. I was thus entertained one summer by a Small White and two Small Coppers that made their abode among the flowers of my window-box garden in London. The White chose a white petunia, on the flower of which it roosted every night, perfectly disguised as a petal. The Coppers gave not one look at my stocks or pinks but settled down on the marigolds, which matched their wings more exactly than any wild flower.

Ingenious as is the mimicry practised by caterpillars and butterflies, it seems that they are only partly successful in duping their enemies, and that a large proportion come to an untimely end. A butterfly sometimes lays as many as 300 to 380 eggs, and as the population remains about the same from year to year, it follows that only one or two of each brood survive. Earwigs are partial to butterfly's eggs; beetles and birds prey on the caterpillars and, of course, some also fall victims to the onslaught of the ichneumon fly (18, 19), and other parasitic insects. A chrysalis is a welcome change of fare to a field mouse; and eggs, caterpillars and chrysalises run the risk of being trampled to death by sheep, cattle and human beings. Let me therefore urge you, when in the country, to walk circumspectly, lest you unwittingly destroy some all too local species. We cannot all carry the broom with which the holy man of India sweeps the path before him lest he destroy life, but we *can* be careful.

It would take an army of hikers and many flocks of sheep to exterminate the Skipper tribe that swarms on grasslands and by the wayside in June, July and August. The Skippers are the gnomes of the butterfly world, and its link with the fantastic world of moths. There is more of the moth than of the butterfly's appearance in their thick bodies and stubby wings, in their buzzing flight and in the posture which they assume whilst resting. Their antennæ are not clubbed in butterfly fashion, but thickened at the tip, and the caterpillar is unlike that of any other butterfly in that it spins a cocoon. The Skippers belong to the family *Hesperiidae*, which has the practical use of all six legs.

These elves atone for their ugliness by their exemplary lives. Among the four grass-eating species of Skippers, for instance, the female butterfly evinces the tenderest care for her eggs, which she deposits for protection within the sheath of the grass. The young caterpillar, which hatches in August, sensibly makes provision against the cold by wrapping itself in a

---

[1] There is a record, in the *Entomologist*, of this butterfly feeding from phlox in a garden.

29　Grizzled Skipper, *Pyrgus malvae*

[*Magnification* × 2

30　Ringlet, *Aphantopus hyperantus*

[*Magnification* × 2

31 Purple Emperor, *Apatura iris*

[*Magnification* × 2

cocoon, in which it hibernates through the winter. Emerging in May, it chooses a grass-blade, across which it spins silken cords that contract when dry and draw the edges of the leaf together in the form of a tube. In this snug shelter it lives until the time arrives for it to spin its pupal cocoon, coming out only to feed; and so that it shall not foul its abode, Nature has equipped it with a springed apparatus by means of which it flicks the ejected excrement out of the doorway of its home.

The common brown and tan Large Skipper, *Ochlodes venata*, flies in company with the fawn-coloured Small Skipper, *Thymelicus sylvestris*. On the East coast, among dunes and banks, is to be found the very similar Essex Skipper, *Thymelicus lineola*, first recognised as a distinct species in 1899. The Lulworth Skipper, *Thymelicus acteon*, is olive in hue and was discovered in Lulworth Cove in 1832; it still frequents sheltered spots along the Dorset coast.

I know of wooded chalk hills in Wiltshire where fly, in June, the not uncommon Dingy Skipper, *Erynnis tages*, a mouse-coloured creature, the caterpillar of which feeds on the trefoil, and the Grizzled Skipper, *Pyrgus malvae* (29), whose name is more suggestive of a weather-beaten sea captain than of the chequered little black and white butterfly that skips among the rockrose and thyme. Its caterpillar feeds on woodland plants—the bramble and the wild strawberry.

The rarity of this family is the Chequered Skipper, *Carterocephalus palaemon*, a woodland butterfly. The Silver-spotted Skipper, *Hesperia comma*, is found locally on chalky hills in the south of England, and here and there elsewhere. These conclude the list of these curious insects.

CHAPTER VIII

The Woodlands

THE haunts of butterflies are determined by the soil, and the plants that grow on it. Limestone, chalk, and sandy soils are particularly rich in plants favoured by butterflies and their caterpillars, those localities where soils mingle being especially good hunting-grounds. In a valley in Wiltshire, where the chalk merges into the lower greensand, I have found as many as thirty-two kinds of butterflies within a radius of two and a half miles.

Among the wild flowers sought after by butterflies—by the Peacock, White Admiral, Painted Lady, the large Fritillaries, and the hedgerow Satyrs in particular—the blackberry and the thistle have first place. Their nectar appears to be particularly sweet and abundant and is easy of access by reason of the shape of the flowers, which provide also a comfortable foothold; while the spears and grappling-hooks with which leaves and stems are armed protect and isolate the plant, whose guests feed undisturbed, secure in their flowery fortress.

Hemp agrimony is another plant attractive to Peacocks. The Small Copper's favourites are the ragwort and fleabane; Orange-tips frequent "honesty" in gardens, with cow-parsley and hedgerow flowers; Spring Fritillaries and Brimstones sip nectar from the bugle and bluebells. Blues, Skippers and Small Heaths love knapweed, scabious and wild carrot, while the late-flowering ivy attracts, in October, the last of the Red Admirals, Small Tortoiseshells and Peacocks of field and wayside prefer to sit on the warm ground, but in gardens they visit the buddleia, scabious, statice, heliotrope, Michaelmas daisy and that other daisy known as "black-eyed Susan", in company with their cousins, the Red Admirals, Peacocks and Painted Ladies.

A knowledge of soils and plants is useful, but it is not an infallible guide. Butterflies are often unaccountably absent from a locality where plants and aspect combine, one would think, to afford a "desirable residence", while in some comparatively unattractive spot near by, they abound. Thus was I, one day, surprised and delighted to discover, in a barren, sun-baked, rabbit-mined hollow of the downs, a colony of Dark Green Fritillaries, *Argynnis aglaia* (Plate VI). Their caterpillars feed on the violets that grow among grass on the hillsides. A butterfly chooses the hottest place he can find, for he is a creature of the sun and his daily awakening and activity and powers of flight correspond to the strength of its rays. You will see this sun-worshipper resting on the ground, whose refracted heat toasts him underneath, while his flattened wings absorb, from above, the beneficent rays of his divinity.

PLATE VI.

Top left: SMALL PEARL BORDERED FRITILLARY.   *Top right:* DARK GREEN
FRITILLARY.   *Middle left:* DARK GREEN FRITILLARY, UNDERSIDE.   *Middle
right:* SILVER-WASHED FRITILLARY, UNDERSIDE, FEMALE.   *Lower left:* SILVER-
WASHED FRITILLARY, MALE.

We too love the sun: but we can have enough even of a good thing. Let us therefore seek the welcome half-shade of the woodlands, where are to be found, in July, a galaxy of beauties; White Admirals (Frontispiece, Plate I, and 34), Fritillaries that rival them in grace, and Purple Hair-streaks, the females of which reflect the royal colour of that monarch among our butterflies, *Apatura iris*, the rare and splendid Purple Emperor.

Emperor, *Apatura iris* (31), and "Empress" have a lovely buff-streaked underside that simulates a shadow, but she lacks the purple sheen on the upper surface that makes him such a coveted prize and gives him his classical title of Iris and his Continental name of "Large Lustre Butterfly".

Both the male and female butterfly live high aloft on an oak-tree throne, round which they circle on widespread, velvety wings. The "Empress" never descends to earth, but the Emperor is an inquisitive butterfly, and can be attracted to the ground by spreading a newspaper under the tree, or by flashing a mirror upwards. Like several other butterflies, it is fond of the juices of decaying meat and has been seen alighting on a game-keeper's "gibbet" in a wood. It is also partial to a damp cow-pat.

Entomologists of bygone days used to pursue this butterfly with a net mounted on a twenty-foot pole. They now adopt the simpler method of luring it to earth.

The Purple Emperor was formerly to be found in Wales, in Huntingdon-shire, in the New Forest and in the Chattenden Woods of Kent. Now it occurs in reduced numbers here and there, in large oak-woods; chiefly in the New Forest and in Huntingdonshire. It is possible that the decrease of this beautiful butterfly may be due to the birds which probably find out the hibernating caterpillars in winter.

The caterpillars of the Purple Emperor feed on the sallow. They are uncommonly like green slugs, complete with horns, at this period of their existence. They hibernate during the winter in a fork of a branch or on sallow leaves which they lash to the twig with silken bonds that with-stand autumn fall and the storms of winter. Waking in spring-time, they complete their meal, and become green chrysalises whose form and mark-ings imitate the curves and veins of the sallow leaf from which they hang.

If by unhappy chance the Purple Emperor should become extinct, there will of course be claimants to the throne. Naturalists will form factions, one of which, the Papilionists, will advocate the accession of the Swallow-tail (22); while the Fritillarians (of whom I shall be one) will contend, with some truth, that the Swallow-tail has too many foreign relations to be a suitable monarch, and that our Silver-washed Fritillary, *Argynnis paphia* (Plate VI), is as regal a creature and one belonging to a family well represented in our island. Its caterpillar feeds on that most English of plants, the violet; and is not the butterfly already apparelled in royal robes of silver?

I have spent unforgettable days in the July woods, watching the soarings

6

and alightings of this beautiful butterfly. Slowly it steps over the bramble blossoms, whose nectar it loves, probing them with its delicate proboscis Proudly it struts and flaunts, chasing away an impudent bluebottle who has dared to approach. Deliberately it flattens his leopard-spotted wings to the sun, and the down on its back glistens like gold. The Queen is distinguished from the King by her ochreous yellow colour, larger size, and heavier dark markings. A moment more, and a dusky form sails down —it is the dark, uncommon variety of the female—Valezina, an elegant creature with wings of black and olive, tinged with green.

The female fritillary lays her eggs in crevices of the bark of trees (usually oaks), not far from the ground and always in woods where dog-violets grow. The tiny caterpillar (33) hatches in August, makes a meal off the top of its egg-shell and spends the autumn and winter in a chink of the tree, without food and protected only by the bark. In spring-time, its spark of life rekindles and impels it to the hazardous journey from tree to ground, over twigs which are to it logs, and clods of earth unsurmountable as boulders. The persevering mite eventually finds the dog-violet plants which are to be its food, among which it grows to be a fine spiny horned caterpillar which in its turn becomes a rugged brown chrysalis, suspended from a nearby twig.

The Silver-washed Fritillary is local to the south and west of England. I have seen it in Wiltshire, but its chief haunt seems to be the New Forest, where it is still very plentiful.

Our other woodland Fritillary, the High-Brown, *Argynnis cydippe*, can be identified at a glance by its underwings. In contrast to Paphia's green and silver-streaked brocade, these have a buff-coloured background studded with pearls, larger and more lustrous than the gems that adorn the moss-green underwings of the Dark-green Fritillary. All three butterflies are remarkable for their swift and powerful flight. When feasting, *Paphia* is approachable, but *Cydippe* remains shy and wary to a degree. How often, on wooded Cotswold hillsides, have I stalked the elusive creature, only to give up the chase, hot and cross and stung by nettles. In Wiltshire, I have watched the female laying her eggs on leaves of the violet; and I have noticed that the butterflies keep together, in pairs, in a defined patch of woodland, or sunny glade, where the couple are daily to be found during a period of, perhaps, two or three weeks.

Cydippe's egg is laid in July and August. It matures during the autumn, but the fully formed spiny caterpillar wisely elects to remain in its domed cradle throughout the cold winter, hatching in spring when violet leaves provide its succulent salad.

New Forest glades haunted in spring by Selene are in July the home of another wonder of nature: *Limenitis camilla*, the White Admiral (Frontis-piece and 34), or White Admirable of the older entomologists. When I behold this Sybil,[1] my allegiance to the fritillaries wavers, and I ask myself

---

[1] Camilla was formerly known as Sybilla.

32   Caterpillar of Small Copper Butterfly, *Lycaena phlaeas*

[*Magnification* × 4

33   Caterpillar of Silver-washed Fritillary, *Argynnis paphia*

[*Magnification* × 2

34 White Admiral Butterfly, *Limenitis camilla*

whether darkest velvet brown banded with white, and underwing pencilling of umber and faintest blue, are not alliances more subtle even than leopard-spots and pearls?

The White Admiral is one of two species of butterfly—the other being the Comma—that have become commoner of recent years. It is spreading all over the south of England.

Very curious is this Admiral's egg, the hexagonally pitted surface of which imitates, in miniature, the honeycomb of the bee. The single-brooded caterpillar, which hibernates and feeds on the honeysuckle, is conspicuous for its prominent and irregular spines, while the gilding and silvering of the angular chrysalis render it a most decorative object.

Purple Emperor, White Admiral and Fritillaries (of which only two, the rare Queen of Spain and the Niobe Fritillary, are migrants), belong to the family *Nymphalidae*, which includes also the Comma, the Large and Small Tortoiseshell, the Peacock and the migrant Painted Lady, Red Admiral and Camberwell Beauty. Male and female members of this family use only their two hinder pairs of legs, the front pair being rudimentary, but they do not appear to be inconvenienced by this pedestrian limitation.

Those smaller woodland butterflies, allies of the Blues, the Hairstreaks, are easily overlooked by a beginner, for their colours are subdued and their arboreal habits render them inconspicuous. The short tails that adorn their hind wings give them the appearance of dapper little people dressed in tail coats. Rarity confers a distinction on the Black Hairstreak, *Strymonidea pruni*, which is, I believe, only found in Monk's Wood in Huntingdonshire, where it feeds on the blackthorn, with a chrysalis like a bird-dropping. The green caterpillar of the rather scarce Brown Hairstreak, *Thecla betulae* (24), feeds not on the birch, as its name would lead one to expect, but on the sloe. It is described as flying among oak-trees in the south and east of England, and as far north as Lancashire and Westmorland. I have an acquaintance with the not uncommon Purple Hairstreak, *Thecla quercus*. Its colour and high-flying habits imitate those of the Purple Emperor. The sea-urchin-like egg—which lies dormant for seven or eight months—is laid on twigs of the oak, on the leaves of which the caterpillar feeds and to which the chrysalis is lashed; while the butterfly feasts, it is supposed, on the honey-dew that they exude, for it never settles on flowers. Like the Purple Emperor, it can be tempted from its oak-tree perch by a lure of rotten meat.

The prettiest member of the group is, I think, the White-letter Hairstreak, *Strymonidea w-album* (p. 41). Its cumbersome name refers to the initial of white bordered by orange, apparent near the tail on the olive underside of the lower wings. The upper surface is uniformly dark, thus differing from the orange-blotched wings of the Brown Hairstreak. I have seen this sprightly little butterfly swarming on the sweet flower-spikes of the privet, in a wooded dell in the Cotswolds, where sheltered warmth and a carpet of wild flowers afford a Paradise for butterflies. Let us travel on to this country of the west, and when we tire of its woody ravines and hidden streams we can escape on to the brow of the hill, and feel the breeze, and watch the shadows scudding over the ripening corn. And in these pleasant places let us not forget the meed of admiration due to that brilliant little creature, ally of the Blues and Hairstreaks, the Small Copper, *Lycaena phlaeas*. More prolific than the single-brooded Hairstreaks, it produces three and sometimes four broods in a summer. The egg has the sea-urchin appearance characteristic of the family, and the caterpillar (32), which hibernates, feeds on the sorrel and on the dock, thereby bestowing a claim to interest on this dullest of weeds. You will find this burnished butterfly all over England—on heaths, by the wayside, and even on waste ground round factories and railway sidings. It is in no danger of undergoing the eclipse which has been the unfortunate fate of its ally, the splendid Large Copper, *Lycaena dispar*, which was formerly abundant in the fen district of East Anglia. There is no doubt that this butterfly's disappearance is partly due to the greed of collectors. Rural workers in the fens found that the butterflies had a money value, and sold them at prices varying from £1 to £20. Specimens caught in 1847 at Holme Fen are believed to be the last native butterflies seen alive in this country; but a rather similar species has lately been re-established by members of the Royal Entomological Society, London, who imported a small number of specimens from Holland to Wicken Fen. This original importation has now increased and forms a thriving colony secure from the ravages of collectors and from the inroads of golf-links, jerry-building and agriculture.

East Anglia is the home of another splendid butterfly: *Nymphalis polychloros*, the Large Tortoiseshell (35). During the spring and late summer of 1941 and 1942 I watched *Polychloros* in its haunts on the Essex–Suffolk border. The butterflies appeared first in April, feeding from the flowers of the Butterbur, *Petasites officinalis*, in company with Small Tortoiseshells: *polychloros* and *urticae* played together, turning aerial somersaults and flying to and fro in figure-of-eight patterns. A male *polychloros* was apparently trying to copulate with a female *urticae*, creeping over her and fanning his wings in quick motion. She awaited him with the tip of her body upturned.[1] The male then left her and did not return, so that I did not see the upshot of this strange courtship. Then, on July 1st 1942, *polychloros* caterpillars appeared in a wooden shed in my garden, about twenty yards from an elm thicket in a hedge, and about 150 yards from a large elm-tree, one or the other having presumably been their food supply. The caterpillars crept up to the overhead beams and there suspended themselves to pupate. I watched the convulsions of one as its skin split. The protuberances of the chrysalis appeared suddenly through a rent in the underside of the caterpillar's skin, which was then shrugged upwards. Unfortunately I could not watch the final discarding. I kept three pupæ from which butterflies emerged on July 20th, 21st, and 22nd respectively.

[1] A "defence" attitude? See the following chapter.

White-letter Hairstreaks, *Strymonidea W-album*, on Bramble
(*Life-size*)

Polychloros was abundant in my neighbourhood throughout late July and August 1942, its favourite haunt being a certain dead elm-tree from which most of the bark had been stripped by hornets. Here, on the bare, weather-whitened wood, eight or ten would sit of an afternoon, flattened against the tree or slowly fanning their wings, while round them the busy hornets proceeded with their work of demolition. Seen thus the tree presented a curious and beautiful appearance; one could liken it to a pillar of marble inlaid with metal and encrusted with precious stones. *Polychloros* likes to sit, wide-winged, in the roadway, in the glare of the sun; or, with closed wings, on the bare earth. When clouds obscure the sun, I have seen him flutter up the walls of a cottage and creep into a hole in the thatch.[1]

[1] I have to acknowledge to N. D. Riley, Esq., F.R.E.S., F.Z.S., editor of *The Entomologist*, the permission to reprint these notes on *Polychloros*. They appeared in the *Entomologist*, February 1943, vol. LXXVI, No. 957, page 30.

35 Large Tortoiseshell, *Nymphalis polychloros*

[*Magnification* × 2

36 Red Admiral Butterfly, *Vanessa atalanta*, on a Honey-pot

[About half life-size

CHAPTER IX

Grey Days: Some Notes on the Courtship of Butterflies

GREY days have their charm for those of us who watch butterflies; for it is then that we see them resting and observe the leaf-shapes of their folded wings. Then, too, if the season be ripe and atmospheric conditions favourable, we may watch that prettiest of all ceremonies, the butterflies' courtship and love-flight. This matrimonial rite takes place at certain times of day that vary with the different species. Thus, the Whites, physically adapted to colours and not to light and darkness, fly early in the day, retire before sundown for the night, and mate in the early afternoon. Ringlets (Plate V), and Speckled Woods (Plate V), mate at midday and in the afternoon, Wall butterflies in the later afternoon; while the swift-flying *Nymphalidae* keep later hours. Their vision is adapted to light and darkness as well as to colours, and they continue their activities through daylight well on into the evening, flying at sunset, mating sometimes at sundown, and even, I am told, in the deepening dusk.

Butterflies are exceedingly sensitive to barometric pressure, as well as to heat and cold, dryness and humidity. These factors influence their physiological processes as well as their diurnal activity. We think of them as creatures of the sun, for, with the exception of the speckled wood (and, perhaps, the green-veined White) they fly, play and feed in sunshine. But for the business of courtship and mating they often prefer a different climate; sultry days, thunder-weather, and the steamy warmth after rain.

The love-flight most easily observed is that of the Cabbage Whites, Large and Small (Plate II), for they are common everywhere in lanes and kitchen gardens in July and August, drifting hither and thither like summer snow. The Small White is neither shy nor wary, nor does it seem particularly sensitive to vibrations or to the human footfall. Let us approach, and see, at close quarters, the ritual of love.

Watching the eddying butterflies, we notice different rythms in their flight. There is the leisurely progress of the butterfly in search of nectar. Flying a foot or more from the ground, it makes a zigzag course, like a tiny ship tacking into the wind. Three, five butterflies rise and soar upwards, wreathed in the tumbling flight of play. Then, as the afternoon becomes sultry, a male and female detach themselves from the medley and begin a more measured dance. It is the courtship flight, the prelude to mating.

I watch, with delight, the aerial pattern of this love-flight, which has something of the quality of music in its pulsing rhythm. The butterflies, flying with quick wing-beats, describe a set figure, following one another in a continuously repeated pattern. Another pair begins to dance. Their

43

choreography follows the same pattern, the same spacing, the loops of their spiral progress becoming smaller as the climax approaches. The courting pairs rise high into the air. For a moment they are lost to sight. Suddenly the female sinks down, followed by the male. Clinging to a grass-blade, she vibrates her wings. Her suitor, arrested in mid-air, hovers over her as though suspended on an invisible wire. His fanning wings announce the finale of the dance. He sinks towards his bride. There is a fluttering, an adjustment of position so quickly executed that the actual joining of the bodies is difficult to see; and the paired butterflies rest. Two creatures have become one; a folded shape like a white flower, tipped by the stamen-like antennæ.

A female Large White, *Pieris brassicae*, to escape from the attentions of a male, flutters down with closed wings and simulates a leaf. The male loses her and flies away
(*Rather less than life-size*)

It is on overcast, windless afternoons in August that the time is ripe for the pairing of the Large White. You will find the couples among foliage — often among bramble leaves in a hedge. Their pale, closed wings resemble the whitish undersides of the leaves among which they rest. And in some leafy lane, or on the warm earth of the kitchen garden, you may often see a quiescent female Large White. She rests with drooping wings and abdomen tilted upwards almost at right angles to her thorax. To her may come an amorous male. He flutters over her, alights on her and attempts to copulate; but she shakes him off, flutters a little way and sinks down with closed wings in the shelter of foliage, where her leaf-shape is a perfect disguise. The baulked suitor flies to and fro, looking for her; discovers her, and again attempts to pair. She escapes again, this time reclining flat among the foliage like a fallen leaf. Now the male has lost her; up and down he searches, but in vain; then he gives up the quest and flies off in search of another bride.

I have observed this hide-and-seek among Small Whites in a bramble hedge. Here the female slipped away under a branch and flew off. The male evidently could not see her departure, and flew up and down the hedge, "quartering" it methodically, and sometimes alighting on the underside of a bramble leaf which he seemed to mistake for the female butterfly. Eventually he too flew away.

I have watched variations of this performance throughout successive summers, but I have never observed this singular posture of the female to be followed by copulation. Rather does it seem to be an attitude of defence, a protection against the untimely advances of the male, who cannot obtain the necessary foothold on the female's body owing to its upright tilt.[1] One scientist[2] is of the opinion that the leaf-shape and fluttering flight of various butterflies is a mimicry designed to protect

Large White male, *Pieris brassicae*, trying, unsuccessfully, to pair with a female
(Less than life-size)

the female from the unwelcome attentions of the male; unwelcome in that, perhaps, she is not yet ripe for mating, or that she has already been paired to her full capacity. Everyday observations in the kitchen-garden certainly confirm this theory, as do also the observations of Dr. Ilse with regard to a foreign Papilio butterfly. The female Papilio hid from the pursuing male in much the same manner that I have here described.

Experiments with paper models have shown that Cabbage White males (Plate II), when ready to mate, will respond to artificial objects of a

[1] I have seen this position in female moths to be followed by copulation with the male. Naturalists will confirm this. Butterflies are, however, so differently adapted that the contrary may quite probably be true with regard to their mating habits. I should be glad of further information on this subject.

[2] Dr. Martin Hering, *Biologie der Schmetterlinge, Liebespiel und Begattung.*

size corresponding to that of the real female.[1] Her scent, her shape, her characteristic pattern (dark spots on a white background), seem to have little relevance.[2] Cabbage Whites have been seen trying to mate with dead males of another species of the same genus, and in the absence of their females, with white snapdragon flowers in a garden. I have seen a male green-veined White chasing a floating petal of apple-blossom. As the petal touched the ground, the butterfly alighted, fluttering his wings and making the trampling movements of the feet that, with White butterflies, precede copulation.

When paper models were used in experiments with Cabbage Whites, it was noticed that the butterflies preferred the yellowish tinge of proof paper to the pure white of filter paper, though the difference is, to our eyes, slight.[3] (Here it may be pertinent to remark that newly emerged Cabbage Whites, especially the females, are tinged with a lovely yellow tint that suffuses the lower under-surface; this yellow colour fades away when the butterflies are dead.)

From these notes—which may be supplemented by scientific informa-tion—it seems evident that the Large and Small Cabbage Whites, and probably other Whites also, rely on their sight, not on their sense of smell, to guide them to their mates.

Grey days in August are auspicious also to the mating of the *Satyrid* butterfly, the Wall. It is, as a rule, a sun-loving creature; yet for its court-ship and mating it, too, awaits late afternoon with the overcast sky, the falling barometer that heralds rain. When ready to pair the female clings, with outspread wings, to an upright grass-blade or stem. The male flutters over her, then drops into the grass and waits awhile beside her, with wings half-opened, before resuming his advances. Male and female flutter together on to the ground for their mating. One naturalist has seen a courting pair of Wall butterflies "butting" one another with their heads and antennæ.

The courtship of the Small Tortoiseshell (Frontispiece, Plate I) seems to be a protracted and elaborate ritual, of which I have never been able to witness the conclusion. In early spring, the Small Tortoiseshells newly emerged from hibernation perform a soaring love-flight that takes the pairs upwards in a spiral course far above the tops of the wayside elms and chestnuts. I have never seen an alighting pair, and surmise that they then fly for some distance high above the earth in a horizontal course before descending. Pairs of the summer brood may be seen, on the hot dusty road or on a tree-stump. Their posturings remind me of the behaviour of courting cats. Male and female rest, motionless at first, near one another, with outspread wings. Then he makes a series of little runs, approaches the females and taps her body with his antennæ. She quivers her wings

---

[1] See Dora Ilse's *The Colour-vision of Insects*, page 102.   [2] Dora Ilse's observations.
[3] See *The Colour-vision of Insects*, by Dora Ilse.

and runs a few inches farther on. He runs after her and the play repeats itself. Then the pairs remain motionless for, perhaps, half an hour. I am told that the actual pairing takes place after dark.

On a chill, windy evening in mid-June (8.30 D.S.T.), I watched the wild love-flight of a pair of Painted Ladies and its consummation. The couple concerned careered to and fro, in a figure-of-eight pattern, close to the ground. They kept to a regular "beat" by the roadside, never flying over the hedge. Now and then they alighted for a moment, then resumed their dance. Finally they subsided together in a leafy nook under a branch, and crept together, with closed wings, side by side. The actual act of copulation was performed without a tremor under the shelter of their wings, and was therefore not to be observed; but the butterflies must have twisted their bodies almost at right angles to their usual position in order to join them. Rain threatened and I went

Mating pair of Wall Butterflies, *Pararge megera* (*About life-size*)

on my way, leaving the pair quiescent; two dusky triangles, like faded leaves.

I have observed, among certain butterflies not usually gregarious, a tendency to collect together for their pairing. Two such instances stand out in my memories of summer days. One is the recollection of a swampy, windless hollow between steep hills, where grew a grove of spotted orchids, tall as the horse-tail that bore them company. Thick woods hid the sky-line, but not the sun, which drew up vapours, and a stagnant smell. Here it was that the courting Ringlets came from the adjacent wood, to flutter their little love-dance and then to hang, coupled, among the orchid flowers and the horsetail spines. Not often were they so to be seen, their usual haunt being a bramble thicket higher up the hill. But I made a note of two days in the summers of 1940 (between 3 and 5 o'clock D.S.T.) and of one thundery afternoon in July 1941, when I counted dozens of pairs in copulation within the radius of a few square yards. The sultry weather, with the humidity of the dell, evidently created conditions that quickened the procreative urge.

Another dell there appears in my mind's eye; a woodland place, running down to a tiny pond. Here are early purple orchids, among a maze of woodruff and the cuckoo-flowers that are as transitory as the sunshine of May. This is the nuptial bower of the Green-veined Whites, which con-gregate from the surrounding wood here, and here only, for their mating.

The Green-veined White (Plate II) likes moist surroundings: the Common Blue (Plate IV) dry ones. I am interested in a colony that shows a preference for a bank covered with tall rough grass, knapweed and straggling scabious. The Blues perch, with tilted wings, to feed from the cushioned flowers, and congregate before sundown to cling and sleep on the stems of the grasses.

The summer brood of *Icarus* has been out on the downs since July 31st, the males being first on the scene; but this particular colony appears about August 13th. During a few days of settled fine weather males and females fly low among the grasses, as far as I can see mating not at all. But on August 21st, the barometer falls. A haze obscures the sun and the wind changes, coming in gusts that portend rain. Visiting the bank that afternoon at four o'clock (D.S.T.) I see what appear to be thin trails of blue-grey vapour rising from the grass. The Blues (Plate IV) are per-forming their love-flight.

One after another the pairs (which had seemingly chosen their partners before my arrival) soar vertically upward to a height of eight or nine feet. Then the pairs whirl along, parallel to the ground, in a jerky progress like the text-book delineation of a short wave-length. By running after them I keep pace with one pair and witness the completion of the flight. This couple, blown somewhat out of its course by the rising wind, eventu-ally descends, and comes to rest on a stunted thorn, where, after a final skirmish, copulation takes place. Their movements are so quick that I am unable to see the adjustment and joining of the bodies; but the pairs rest tip to tip, as do the Whites and Satyrids. When the paired butterflies fly after copulation, the male Common Blue carries the female.

The Chalk-hill Blue male likewise carries the female, while the females of the Meadow Brown, the Wall Butterfly, and the Small Heath carry the males. I have so far not been able to observe whether the same habit prevails among other Satyrid butterflies.

It seems evident that something other than a similarity of age causes the simultaneous mating that you too may have noticed in Ringlets, Green-veined Whites and Common Blues. Everyday observations of butterflies illustrate the statements of science—namely, that weather will hasten, or defer, the maturity and subsequent egg-laying of butterflies. One recently emerged may, barometric conditions permitting, quickly attain the same physiological state as another, older perhaps by a few days, which has been suspended in its function by unpropitious weather. Thus butterflies of different ages may mate at the same time. The effect of the weather is less apparent in double-brooded, Wall butterflies, or in the continuously-brooded Meadow Brown, because the life-spans of the broods overlap. But with the simple brood of the Ringlet, that lives only through a July, this collective mating is noticeable. As fruit is ripened by the sun and rain, so these living bodies are ripened by humidity and heat. Attuned to the elements in a way that we can but dimly apprehend, obedient to what laws we know not, this population, in the fullness of time, is gathered together to celebrate the festival of love.

The anatomical devices that effect the mating of butterflies are ingenious in their structure. Those of the male consist of an intromittent organ, protruding from the tip of his body, and reinforced by an array of levers and pincers which enable him firmly to grasp the abdomen of the female. Her copulatory opening, placed somewhere in the region of her eighth segment, receives the male organ, and through it, the fertilising sperm. This passes through the female's body down a tube, or duct, of varying lengths in the various species, into a purse-like sac, in which it is stored until required. Between the copulatory orifice and the storage sac, the duct opens into another passage, which in its turn leads into the oviduct. This oviduct is the thoroughfare down which the eggs, when ripe, pass from the ovaries to their own exit at the end of the body; an exit quite distinct from the copulatory orifice.

And here we notice one of Nature's most orderly arrangements. Matters are so contrived that the sperm transmitted by the male is packed in a flask-like capsule of exactly the right shape and size to fit into the storage sac. From the neck of the capsule the sperm passes into a secondary receptable, from which it is squeezed, by muscular pressure, little by little, as required, into the oviduct, where it comes into contact with the eggs released from the ovaries, and fertilises them.[1]

---

[1] This is a generalised description of a complicated process carried out by elaborate structures that vary in the different species of butterflies and moths.

Fertilisation of the eggs may not take place till long after copulation. Usually it occurs just before the eggs are laid. The mating butterflies often remain paired for many hours, held together by the genital structures, while the transfer of sperm takes place. In the foreign butterfly, *Pernassius*, the hypertrophied accessory glands of the male produce a secretion that hardens and cements the pair together for the necessary period.[1]

All butterflies are influenced in their egg-laying by temperature. The females of some species lay next day, and some continue to lay for five or six weeks if the eggs are laid singly. Others lay many eggs in a batch on the same day. The eggs of the Large White hatch in 8 to 10 days after being laid; most of the Small White in 3 days in hot weather, 7 days in temperate weather; those of the Ringlet in 18 days; eggs of the Wall butterfly in about 10 days; the Common Blue's eggs in 9 days, while those of the Chalk-hill Blue remain dormant for 230 days before the caterpillars emerge.

Butterflies are unable to assimilate protein, and as it forms part of the substance of the egg, this necessary substance has to be carried over from the caterpillar stage and stored in the pupa and then in the body of the perfect insect. Consequently the abdomen of a freshly emerged female butterfly is, as you may have observed, large.[2]

In butterflies (and in some moths) with a long imaginal life there are very few fully developed eggs in the ovaries at the time of the insect's emergence. Most of them are matured during the life of the butterfly. But in some moths, *Bombycids* and *Lymantrids*, that, possessing no mouthparts, are unable to feed, all the required eggs are ripe in the moth's body at the time of its emergence from the pupa.[3]

The structure of the genital organs is differently formed in different species of butterflies, but is in each species constant; much more so than the markings on the wings. Classification is based largely upon the form of these organs, which are sometimes the most differently shaped in species where the wing-patterns are the most alike, as for instance, in some Noctuid Moths.[4] The reason for the differentiation of the sexual organs is this: that Nature wishes to keep each species distinct and each type true. For each type has, during the course of ages, evolved its own characteristics, which are of use to it in the life it leads. If one species were to interbreed with another, these peculiarities would be liable to disappear, or to give place to others, useless, or even harmful to the species.[5]

Among moths (which, unlike most butterflies, find each other by scent) the male tends to become dazed and to lose himself in the scent-circle of a female, and to mate with the next female that passes by. The specialised structure of the sexual organs prevents this, and ensures the mating of moths of the same species only.[6]

---

[1] V. B. Wigglesworth: *Principles of Insect Physiology.*   [2] *Ibid.*   [3] *Ibid.*
[4] Dr. Martin Hering, *Biologie der Schmetterlinge, Liebespiel und Begattung.*
[5] *Ibid.*   [6] *Ibid.*

Moths are less highly developed than butterflies and show a greater plasticity; illustrated by their varying wing-patterns, as for instance in the Burnet family. This variability in wing-pattern (and also in size) goes with a variable sex-instinct. Butterflies, on the other hand, may be looked upon as a group where the type has become fixed, and on the whole we do not find so many variations among them as among moths. But a certain plasticity has been retained by the *Lycaenidae* and *Nymphalidae* which show much variation in colour and wing-markings. Among them we find, too, a corresponding variability in their sex instincts; they sometimes pair

Mating Pair of Painted Lady Butterflies, *Vanessa cardui*
(*Rather larger than life*)

with other species. Cross-pairings have been observed among the following butterflies (the partner first indicated being the male): Meadow Brown with Ringlet, Meadow Brown with Small Tortoiseshell, Bath White with Large White, and Common Blue with Chalk-hill Blue.

And now the clouds lift; and as the sun shines out, and the butterflies spread their wings, you may see, in the males of some species, on their upper wing-surfaces, the markings that denote the position of the scent-scales. In the Skippers, these scales form black bars, or crescents, on the upper wing; the curved bar of one Skipper gives its name to Hesperia Comma. The scent of the male Silver-washed Fritillary (Plate VI) is secreted in the three black bars that are so conspicuous on its upper wings. Among the Blues and the Whites, the scent-scales are spread over the surface of the wings.

As a general rule, it is the males of butterflies that carry the scent, secreted in various parts of wings or body, thereby to attract, and subjugate, the females when they have found them. With their swift flight, the females, if not immediately stimulated, might otherwise pass by and miss their suitors. But some female butterflies also carry scent-organs; those of the female *Argynnids* (genus of Fritillaries), are situated between the seventh and eighth ring of the abdomen.[1] Among moths, on the other hand, it is the females that distil the scent, which is secreted sometimes in organs on the legs, sometimes on the sides or near the tip of the abdomen. These moth-females are sluggish in their habits, slow of flight, and content, often, to hang motionless, sending out their scent which attracts the males from afar, and awaiting the arrival of suitors to whom the possession of scent-organs would be superfluous.

· The colours of male butterflies play their part in courtship and mating; and here it is obvious that the most brilliant colouring is to be found in males of the species that can *see* one another; as, for instance, in the Blues, Among moths, that find each other by scent, the difference in colour between the sexes is not so apparent.

Sometimes the scent of butterflies is perceptible to our noses. When "setting" Green-veined Whites (Plate II), I have noticed their scent, that resembles lemon verbena. The Large White is supposed to smell of geranium, the Grayling of chocolate, the Pale Clouded Yellow of pineapple, and the Clouded Yellow of heliotrope.

[1] See Dr. Martin Hering, *Biologie der Schmetterlinge*.

CHAPTER X

Autumn

AUGUST passes slowly. It is a time of waiting; all earth is ripening to the harvest. Peacocks emerge, followed by a second brood of Blues, Speckled Woods, Tortoiseshells, Wall and Cabbage butterflies. Among the creeping creatures a certain activity is apparent; they are already preparing for the winter. Furry caterpillars of moths bustle across garden paths, seeking a nook in which to sleep their pupal slumber. And, unseen by us, in woods and fields and hedges, a myriad other caterpillars creep into the shelter of grass and roots and spin protective webs, or lash themselves to leaves, some to sleep as chrysalises, others to lie dormant until awakened by the warmth of spring. While in this torpid condition they consume less oxygen than when active and remain unharmed by frost and snow. The chrysalises of the Large Copper have an even greater degree of endurance, for they pass the winter submerged in the waters of the fens. Regarding the hibernation of caterpillars, Mr. H. E. Williamson tells of a naturalist known to him who has had made a special thermometer for taking the temperature of flowers and insects. With it he tells if a caterpillar is alive; for when its temperature rises to that of the surrounding air, it is dead.

September brings a glory and a blossoming. It is as if a second spring were here, a faint reflection of the loveliness of May. The sun shines now with a muted quality, as if from behind a veil; he warms where before he scorched. These golden days are linked in my memory with a garden in the West Country, where the autumn butterflies are more splendid than in any other. Tortoiseshells and Peacocks, Red Admirals, female Brimstones[1] and Painted Ladies, jostle each other on the Michaelmas daisies, greedily imbibing the nectar cupped in each tiny chalice of the composite flower. Their bodies are distended with nectar; so absorbed are they that they forgot to be wary and we can look at them closely. They make great play with their antennæ, raising and lowering them and tapping the flowers. When with the aid of this combination of nose and fingers, the butterfly has found a source of nectar, it unfurls its proboscis, which as a rule remains neatly rolled up between the hairy, beak-like palpi, and plunges the tip into the flower. This long and sensitive tongue, apparent to our unaided vision as a tapering hair, is in reality a complicated apparatus consisting of two parallel tubes, which can be unhooked for

[1] Male and female Brimstones usually go into hibernation in August. But July and early August of 1939 were wet and cold and the butterflies could not feed. The males appear to have gone into hibernation at the normal time in spite of this, but the females stayed out later than is their wont, in the warm September sunshine, feeding up for the winter, and perhaps acquiring reserves of strength for the important business of egg-laying in the spring.

cleaning; the inner surface of each is concave, thus forming a central channel up which food passes. The outer tubes are furnished with muscle bands for rolling them up and there are suction muscles inside the butterfly's head. The proboscis of the Painted Lady is white; she has a white face and white legs, which give her a masked, gloved and gaitered appearance. She fans pointed wings, salmon pink with a dark brown pattern above, pearled with white, their underside flushed with rose and marbled with a grey and creamy pattern of the most minute delicacy. The Red Admiral, *Vanessa atalanta* (Frontispiece and 36), flaunting vermilion and black, set off by white spots, is too well known to need description. The old writers pay tribute to the splendour of the "Admirable" to which they give also the name of the Alderman Butterfly. It is excessively fond of overripe fruit; it will come also to trees "sugared" by the moth-collector and to the sugar-pots (36), with which gardeners trap wasps and flies, and it is said that a willow-tree bored by the caterpillars of the goat-moth will attract every Red Admiral in the neighbourhood.

Two Red Admirals rise in mimic combat. One settles on a fallen plum, the other on the earth of the garden border, across which it advances towards its rival in a series of little runs, up hummocks, down hollows, like a painted galleon, all sail set, careering onward through a turbulent sea; and the lesser hulks of basking flies scatter before it. Then the absurd delightful creatures tire of earth and float away with the graceful flight that has earned them the name of Atalanta.[1]

I have seen an old coloured plate depicting a newly emerged "Red Admirable" shedding "three drops of blood". These drops are shed by every moth and butterfly at the moment of hatching: they are an urinary secretion, the residue of the caterpillar's organism. The legends of a "rain of blood" probably have their origin in these drops, shed perhaps by a swarm of migrating butterflies.

The immigrant Red Admirals, whose home was in France, lay their eggs singly on the topmost leaves of the nettle, which the spiny caterpillar draws together into a tent, in which it lives and in which it eventually hangs itself up as a chrysalis (Frontispiece, Plate I, and 37).

Red Admirals are so evocative of an English garden that it is hard to believe that they are not native. It was formerly thought that these lovely and lively butterflies of autumn, offspring of spring immigrants from the Continent, could not withstand the cold and wet of our winters and perished at the first frost. There is now, however, a certain amount of evidence to show that they can survive the winter here in a state of hibernation. A number of these butterflies, looking rather the worse for wear, were recently seen in the month of March, in the Isle of Wight, sunning themselves on the cliffs of a sheltered cove, near some rabbit holes.

[1] The maiden Atalanta, most swift-footed of mortals, required of her suitors that they should run races with her. She was eventually out-run, or rather out-manœuvred: by Milanion, who distracted her attention by rolling three golden apples before her, and she married him.

37 Chrysalis of Red Admiral Butterfly, *Vanessa atalanta*

[*Magnification* × 1½

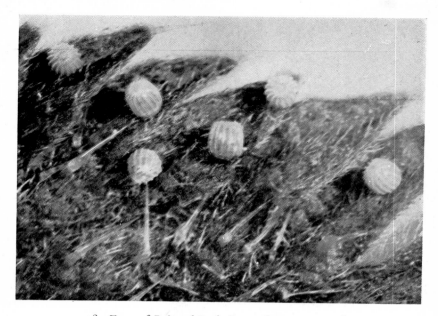

38   Eggs of Painted Lady Butterfly, *Vanessa cardui*

COLOUR: GREEN

[*Magnification* × 20

39   Eggs of Painted Lady Butterfly, *Vanessa cardui*, on Nettle

COLOUR: GREEN, SEVENTEEN WHITISH LONGITUDINAL RIDGES

[*Magnification* × 50

Peacock butterflies hibernate down rabbit holes, and it is probable that these Red Admirals had chosen a similar shelter.

A Red Admiral was seen on March 25th 1940, at Portmeirion, North Wales, and there is a report of another at Harlech on the same day. There are also other records—I have found a limp, newly dead Red Admiral on my garden path in January. It is thought that the species may be building up its resistance and acquiring reserves of strength to last through the winter, and that we may ultimately have a native race of Red Admirals.

There are, too, a number of records supporting the idea of the butterfly's southward return flight. On September 3rd 1938, a naturalist saw Red Admirals flying to and fro on the beach on the south coast of England; occasionally one would fly out to sea, without returning.

This evidence has been substantiated by a lighthouse-keeper at St. Mary's, Scilly Isles, who has on occasions seen Red Admirals and other migrant butterflies, flying from England towards the Continent in autumn.

Red Admiral, *Vanessa atalanta*, feeding on fallen plum
(About life-size)

The home of the Painted Lady (Frontispiece, Plate I) is in the Riviera and North Africa, from where, as I have told you, migrants visit us annually in varying numbers. Some of the butterflies settle down in the south of England, others pass on to the north of Scotland, while some of them reach Iceland.

During the wettest summers on record immense swarms have arrived at intervals. Eggs (38, 39), are usually laid during June, and the butterflies resulting from this brood emerge in August, and produce, in October, a second generation. The fate of the autumn adults is still uncertain and observations are particularly needed to see if they return to the south or die here without having laid eggs.

Thistles and burdock provide food for the caterpillar of the Painted Lady, and the insect is consequently to be found on waste ground and on the downs, as well as in gardens. The female butterfly tests the leaves

of the food plants by "drumming" on them with her rudimentary front
legs.[1]

September brings the jagged butterfly with the complicated family
affairs—the Comma, *Polygonia c-album* (40). It pairs after hibernation and

in April lays eggs on the nettle
and sometimes on the hop.
Thirty or forty per cent of these
eggs—always the first laid—
result in a light-coloured variety
with slightly indented wings,
known as *Hutchinsoni*. But the
remainder of the parents' eggs
have resulted in a brood of
butterflies with a dark and
jagged appearance. It was
always understood that the
Hutchinsoni was the only form
which paired at once, among
themselves, to produce, in September, a second brood of
butterflies of a dark type; and
that the blond *Hutchinsoni's*
dark brothers and sisters did
not pair among themselves, or
with the *Hutchinsoni*, but went
into hibernation until the following spring, when they paired
with the hibernated butterflies
of the second brood. Recent
observations show, however,
that dark types of the first
brood will pair with *Hutchinsoni*, or among themselves.
These various alliances result in
four or five different types of
the butterfly.

Comma, *Polygonia c-album*, on ash-bud,
in early spring
(*Life-size*)

The Comma is aloof in its
habits and does not fly or feast
in mixed company; it marks out
a "beat" in hedgerow or garden,

where it flies rapidly to and fro. It is fond of heliotrope flowers and of a

[1] A film depicting the "drumming" of the Painted Lady has been shown by Dora
Ilse at the Nottingham Meeting of the British Association and also in America. I have
watched a female Painted Lady "drumming" on leaves of the ragwort— which are
not unlike those of a thistle in shape and colour—and then flying from them to a
thistle, where she laid eggs.

rotten plum, and sits with closed wings on the bare earth, against which it is as inconspicuous as a fallen leaf; for its ragged wings, above so brilliantly orange and black, have a sombre underside marked with the white "Comma" that simulates a speck of lime or of lichen, thus completing the butterfly's protective colouring.

Large Tortoiseshell, *Nymphalis polychloros*, sunning on tree-trunk

The autumn days follow one another, still and serene, yet heavy with a melancholy that catches at the heart. The pale sunshine lingers, with the remoteness of a dream, on the quiet hillside. Beeches turn to flame, oaks to rust, elms to palest sulphur: daily the sun describes a lower arc in the sky and the morning mists are daily later dispelled. Then the wind arises, the wind that has lain quiet for so long. It moans behind banks of clouds, then speaks with the voice of a hundred trumpets; trees and plants bow before its onslaught, and the glory of autumn is scattered. Branches break and groan in the tempest. The whirling leaves, like wraiths of departed butterflies, conjure up the elusive shapes of those that I have failed to find; brown and black Hairstreaks, small and dainty, like birch-leaves; Queen of Spain Fritillaries, spreading pointed wings like October beech leaves pearled with rain-drops; and, rarest of all, the Camberwell Beauty, White-bordered, or Mourning Cloak, that sombrely splendid apparition of autumn. All these and others, hover within the possibilities of the future, and with the thought of them comes the planning of new travels; for where, after all, is the interest of a world in which there are no new discoveries to be made?

And now we must return to the city whence we came; the short dark days are upon us, and the autumn rains. The sadness of departure, the sense of finality that the end of summer brings, is tempered by a sense of contentment as we survey our spoils. Gleaming butterflies, carefully set and dried; live chrysalises, knobbed and speckled and angular, that twitch their tails when disturbed; a few treasured leaves studded with eggs which will result in a menagerie requiring constant food and attention; these trophies of an innocent chase recall abiding memories of the English countryside. With them we have acquired a store of beauty, an imperishable treasure which will brighten the days to come. For in a world torn by suffering and strife, it is to Nature that we turn; hers are the enduring values, the eternal verities. The seasons follow their cycles, the creeping and flying creatures pursue their little lives, unconcerned and undeterred by the follies of mankind. And are their lives, after all, so small? They are part of the great plan of the Universe, of the Life that animates all things; they are manifestations of Nature's law of beauty and order, which inspires and guides the spiritual activities of man. When we behold the butterflies, our faith is renewed and we are comforted; for their bright wings embody an idea, and reveal a philosophy.

40 Comma Butterfly, *Polygonia c-album*, on Michaelmas Daisies

[*Very slightly larger than life*

41 Larva of Privet Hawk-moth, *Sphinx ligustri*, fully fed, climbing from one portion of twig to another   [*About life-size*

42 Small Elephant Hawk-moth, *Deilephila porcellus*

[*Magnification* × 2

PART II   MOTHS

CHAPTER XI

Moths

A FLAME was kindled in my imagination by the discovery of a Hawk-moth
caterpillar, and its winged resurrection; a will-o'-the-wisp flame which
has led me on, not to perdition, but into an enchanted world. The
inhabitants of this world lead strange lives; they experience adventure and
change, encounter enemies and embark on travels. Here are giants and
dwarfs; gnomes that dwell inside trees; nymphs of the wood and garden;
creatures of night and of day. There are beings whose wings are their
glory, and wingless hulks. Some carry their ears in their bellies,[1] others
possess tongues longer than their bodies, while others again are doomed
to exist with no tongues, or mouths, at all. They fill our countryside
with a population whose ways provide unending entertainment for those
of us who are curious. Their very names are fantastic; the Emperor;
the Death's Head; the Spring Usher; the Dog's Tooth; the Magpie; the
Annulet; the Pretty Pug; the Rosy Footman; the Small Tabby; the Snout;
the Heart and Dart; the Neglected, and the Doubtful Rustic; the Fan-foot;
Mother Shipton; the Old Lady.

If you wish to become acquainted with these odd beings, you will need
a seeing eye and much zeal and patience. You will have to peer among
the grass, to search tree-trunks and palings. For most of the moths fly
by night, and rest during the day, cunningly hidden from the enemies
that surround them. Concealment is necessary, for they have no weapons
of defence—they possess neither the biting jaws of the spider and the ant,
nor the stilettos that arm the wasps and bees. They are perfectly harmless
insects.

Nevertheless the moth is, sometimes, a potential menace, for it lays
eggs that result in caterpillar pests. The worst of these is, perhaps, the
caterpillar of the Antler Moth, *Cerapteryx graminis*, which feeds on the
roots of grass and sometimes lays bare whole hillsides or meadows. Its
numbers are, fortunately, kept down by the rooks. Other pests are the
Common Swift, *Hepialus lupulina*, the caterpillar of which destroys the
roots of a number of garden plants and wild plants, and the Winter Moth,
Operophtera brumata, which ravages forests and fruit-trees. In oak woods,
you will often see whole acres stripped by the caterpillars of *Tortrix
viridana*, tiny creatures that dangle in mid-air suspended by silken threads.
And of course there is the Clothes Moth, which has been a bane to mankind

[1] Brimstone moth.

59

ever since the days of the ancient Hebrews. (The Clothes Moth belongs to a group of very small moths known as the *Micro-lepidoptera* and does not come into this book, in which space permits me to mention only some of the larger moths, the *Macro-lepidoptera*).

Pests being what they are, it is as well that their enemies take a toll of them. Among these enemies are birds, always ready to pounce, both by day and by night. I have often seen a sparrow, or a spotted flycatcher, chasing a moth, that dodges and twists like a doubling hare, often escaping from its pursuer into a thick bush. Owls add a moth or two to their evening meal—you will find their wings in the pellets of waste matter thrown up by the sated bird. Nightjars have been seen to swoop down on moths, and fish will rise to the small moths that flutter over the surface of streams in company with the mayfly. Bats snap up moths as well as flies; and the hedgehog relishes any live thing—caterpillar, slug or sleepy moth, that he finds on his rambles. And sometimes the flying moth blunders into a spider's web and becomes entangled in the sticky spokes. Their quivering announces the capture to the owner of the web—that many-eyed ogress with the poisoned fangs. She darts from her central lair and dexterously casts line after line round the struggling victim, who is soon trussed up, inert as a mummy. Then she shears off his wings and keeps him, as we should a ham, suspended in her "larder".

The hunted creatures find safety, when at rest, in their resemblance to their chosen background, and in mimicry of natural objects such as twigs, leaves, feathers and bird-droppings. If looked at attentively, the dullest garden fence becomes suddenly and excitingly alive. Here a knot in the wood resolves itself into the humped form of a Noctuid Moth. There a triangle of hanging bark takes shape as a Waved Umber, and an apparent bird-dropping reveals the delicately mottled wings of the Carpet Moth.

Tree-trunks also are a good hunting-ground. On them you may find splendid moths—the Lobster, the Black Arches and the Pine Hawk, and you will marvel at the perfection of their protective colouring. The Pugs, the Waves, and the Carpets and some of the smaller Noctuids sit on brick and stone, and on the leaves of trees, whence a sharp tap will dislodge them.

Many of the Noctuids hide in long grass during the daytime. So does the Common Swift, which wraps its wings tightly round its body when at rest—the queer little bundle looks like a sheath of the grass. And if you are picking strawberries, you will probably disturb the Yellow Underwing, which has a habit of resting among the leaves of the plant and the surrounding straw.

A great many moths hide so cleverly that they would hardly ever be seen were it not that they are attracted to a light. A lamp placed in the open window on a summer night will bring numbers of them buzzing round the shade. Some fall dazed to the floor whence you can collect them next morning. Although fascinated by a lamp, you will never see the moths when the moon is bright, or the night chilly. They fly on

PLATE VII.

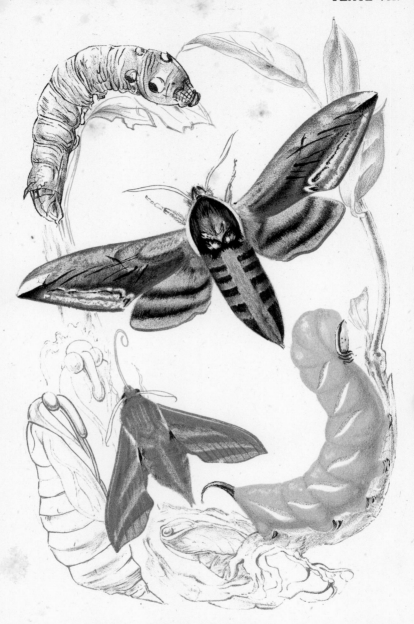

Top left: ELEPHANT HAWK-MOTH CATERPILLAR.   *Upper centre:* PRIVET
HAWK-MOTH.   *Lower left:* ELEPHANT HAWK-MOTH, WITH TWO PRIVET HAWK
PUPAE ON ITS LEFT, AND ITS OWN PUPA BELOW.   *Lower right:* PRIVET HAWK
CATERPILLAR.

cloudy or moonless nights, in thundery weather and before rain. At these times they will come into houses without the lure of a light—probably sensing the coming storm and desirous of shelter.

If the light of a lantern attracts them thus, you can imagine the effect of a lighthouse. The lighthouse-keepers will tell you how they spread sheets every night to collect the swarms of bemused creatures. Our entomological societies work in co-operation with the authorities responsible for the lighthouses, who keep records of the numbers and species captured,[1] among which rarities are sometimes found. In this way valuable informa-tion is acquired concern-ing the habits and, above all, the migration of moths.

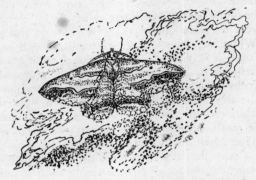

The best way of learn-ing about the ways and the life histories of moths is, of course, to find and rear the eggs and cater-pillars. The eggs can be discovered on the sur-face of leaves, sometimes singly, sometimes in pairs or in clusters. Those of the Hawk-moths are like

Waved Umber, *Hemerophila abruptaria*, on bark
(*Life-size*)

green seed-pearls, the Prominents' are disguised as tiny brown galls, and the Lackeys arrange theirs in an elegant "bracelet" round a twig.

A naturalist tells how he watched a moth laying her eggs on the meshes of a tennis-net. She was followed by an earwig, which gobbled up each egg as soon as laid. The mother took no notice of the brigand and placidly completed her laying. Such creatures of instinct, so devoid of reason, are moths.

The disguises assumed by caterpillars are even more ingenious and curious than those of moths, for having no wings and therefore being unable to escape by flight, they are in need of special protection. The "stick" caterpillars, for instance, are so exactly like twigs, tipped with a bud, that people have been known to frighten themselves very much by grasping them in mistake for a branch. Many caterpillars are armed with weapons, such as an evil-smelling spray that they can eject at will in the face of their enemies; while others are poisonous to the taste, and advertise the fact by their gaudy appearance, and the birds heed the "warning colours" and will not touch them.

Caterpillars of the Oak Eggar and Tiger Moth tribe, when disturbed,

[1] Capt. T. Dannreuther gives a list of 54 species of moths, including a hundred Convolvulus Hawk-moths, taken at a searchlight July–August 1944. (See proof for the *Hastings and East Sussex Naturalist*, Vol. VI, No. 6, May 1945.)

9

roll into a ring and drop off their food-plant into the shelter of the tangled grass and roots below; and so that they be not bruised by the fall, Nature has clothed them with a thick double coating of springy hairs that break their fall and protect their bodies from the impact of thorns and stones.

These hairs are, however, of no avail against the caterpillar's worst enemy, the ichneumon fly (51). The long ovipositor of this fly pierces the hide of any caterpillar, be it furry, spiny, or smooth. The true ichneumon are four-winged insects belonging to the order *Hymenoptera*; there are also parasitic flies with similar habits and with two wings. They belong to the order *Diptera*. Some resemble tiny gnats, others are like the common house-fly, only more hairy, others again resemble wasps. As I have told you, one very small species lays its eggs inside the eggs of the Cabbage White butterfly, and the caterpillar which hatches with the tiny grubs inside it is doomed. Most of these parasitic flies deposit their eggs in the flesh of the living caterpillar, and the gruesome story repeats itself. The grubs drain the juices of the caterpillar and finally emerge, full-fed, from the shrivelled carcase of their host, to spin their own small yellow or white cocoon. Some parasites prey upon one particular species of butterfly or moth, but many more will attack several, or any species. The garden Tiger Moth is attacked by a fly like a bluebottle, only more hairy.

Caterpillars that spin thick cocoons are safe when they reach the pupal stage; for the tough outer covering and the inner case of silk defy attack and are impervious to rain and frost. Perfect safety is also achieved by those that make hard cocoons of bark and glue fixed to the trunk of the tree. Safe cocoons, that blend with their surroundings, are constructed by some species of earth and rubble, on the surface of the ground. But there are many caterpillars that pupate in the crevices of bark, and among moss, protected by the flimsiest of cocoons—mere shreds of silk. These pupæ are easily found out by birds. Others lie underground, quite bare, or encased in a fragile earthern cell; and the mice and moles take their toll of these. You may often see the workings of a mole round the base of a tree. It is useless to dig for pupæ here. Another hunter has forestalled you.

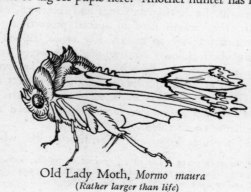

Old Lady Moth, *Mormo maura*
(*Rather larger than life*)

43   Eyed Hawk-moth, *Smerinthus ocellatus*, at rest during the daytime

[*Magnification* × 2]

44 Poplar Hawk-moth, *Laothoe populi*   [*Magnification* × 2

45 Eyed Hawk-moth, *Smerinthus ocellatus*

[*Magnification* × 2

CHAPTER XII

Hawk-moths (Sphingidae)

IN one respect the moths excel the butterflies, and that is in the diversity and magnificence of their caterpillars. The largest and most spectacular of these belong to the Hawk-moths, and the ensuing moths form a splendid family. In Britain there are to be found seventeen species, of which ten are native and seven migratory, most of the latter being very rare.

The Hawk-moths (Plate VII), are exceedingly fast fliers. They are built for speed; their stream-lined, torpedo-shaped bodies afford the minimum of air-resistance and their pointed wings are endowed with an exceptionally strong muscular mechanism, which gives as many as 72 wing-beats to the second.[1] When flying, the moth uses its long abdomen in the same way as a flying bird uses its tail feathers, or a running dog its tail—as a rudder, by means of which it can turn when at full speed. Hawk-moths use their front pair of wings for the movement of flying. The hind pair are used chiefly for gliding.

With the exception of the Death's Head, the Hawk-moths fly at dusk rather than in darkness. Their eyes are very large and their antennæ are curiously shaped—they are thickest in the middle, thence tapering to the base and to the point. Those of the Privet Hawk (Plate VII), are like elongated scrubbing-brushes, their upper surface being convex and rounded and their under-surface flat, toothed with a double array of short spines, or bristles. But the most remarkable feature of the Hawk-moth is its long tongue, which sometimes measures as much as four inches when extended and is specially constructed for sucking nectar from the deep throats of tubular flowers.

The eggs of the Hawk-moths (with the exception of the brown eggs of the Lime Hawk) are green in colour, smooth in texture and oval in shape. They are laid singly, or in twos and threes, usually on the underside of a leaf of the food plant.

Elephant (Plate VII), Lime (46), Eyed (43, 45), Poplar (44), and Privet Hawks (Plate VII), are not uncommon, and when full-fed in August and September the caterpillars are easily found owing to their habit of resting on the outer twigs of their food-plant. The Privet Hawk's, *Sphinx ligustri* (Plate VII), colouring is anything but protective, for the green is much brighter than the colour of the privet leaves on which it feeds and it has, in addition, slanting lilac-and-white stripes and a shiny curved black and yellow horn on its hindmost segment. I can only imagine that the caterpillars (Plate VII), rely for safety on their size and on the disconcerting effect that their expressionless green faces would have on an imaginative bird.

[1] The wing-beats of a butterfly average about nine to the second.

They sit about, like fat jade idols, on their food-tree, clinging to the
twig by their sucker-like hind legs with the front part of their bodies
raised and their faces tucked between their fore-legs, rather in the attitude

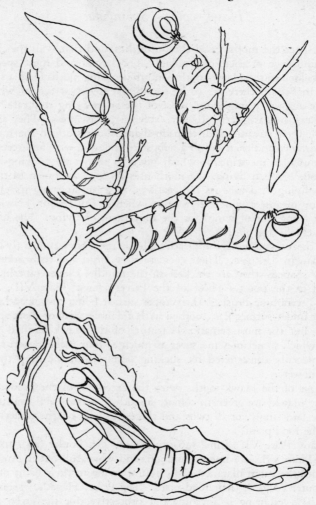

Privet Hawk-moth, *Sphinx ligustri*, Caterpillars and pupa
(Life-size)

of a person praying. An old gardener was once quite put out by seeing a
number of these caterpillars—they had so consequential an air. I find
a few of these creatures every summer and keep them in a cage, especially
designed for their comfort. They enjoy their food; when they are browsing,

the sound of their jaws is like the munching of cows in a meadow. When the times comes for them to pupate, they become restless and their lovely green colour turns to a jaundiced yellow. They refuse food and wander round the earth of their cage, feeling the surface with their forefeet and waving their front segments to and fro in a wild, despairing manner. Then, suddenly, they burrow, and the last that is seen of them is the horn on their tail, waving a farewell as the earth closes over them.[1]

The caterpillar descends to a depth of about four inches and in its final resting-place constructs an earthen cell, the walls hardened with a glue-like cement. In this tomb it sloughs its skin, emerging as a naked, flabby creature like a shell-less shrimp. If disturbed at this critical time, it dies. In a few hours, however, a secretion oozes from the body and hardens into a dark and glossy shell, inside which the moth develops, gradually perfecting the rose and black, the brown and white, of its colouring, its thick soft fur, and the delicate mechanism of limbs and wings, proboscis and antennæ. The pupa can now safely be unearthed and examined. Though not more than an inch and a half long, the thing has the sculptured impassivity, the grandeur, of a sphinx. The rigid form is enwrapped by the wings-to-be, as by a mantle; the lines of their veins and nervures are chiselled on the hard cerements. The eyes are as yet sealed and sightless. From the strangely human face depends a tubular sheath, which encases the proboscis of the future moth. In this guise the creature sleeps its subterranean slumber, and, on a June morning, breaks through the walls of its cell and tunnels upwards to the light.

When free from earth, its shell cracks along the back and round the edges of the wing cases. The antennæ of the moth appear, pressed closely to its sides, and the two round eyes. Then comes a groping leg, and the insect gradually works itself free of its husk and crawls up to the roof of its cage. Here it clings tightly, by all six legs. Its fur is matted; its tiny, crumpled wings hang helpless, as if paralysed. On them appears, in miniature, the imprint of their future design. But the forces of life are at work; the wings slowly unfurl, they expand their membranes and their pattern; they stiffen. The fur of the body dries, and I find in the cage a winged stranger, a downy arrow-shaped creature that parts its strong wings, revealing the rose-and-black striped body beneath. Its face is the face of a squirrel and it carries its antennæ folded along its back, like the ears of a sleeping rabbit. I carry the lovely one into the garden, and with infinite care induce it to walk on to a privet branch. It stamps its delicate feet and quivers its wings as if trying its new-found strength.

[1] A female ligustri brought to me on June 27, 1945, laid eggs, in batches of 2, 3, 16, 16, 15, on the nights of June 29, 30, July 1, 2, 4. The eggs began hatching on July 14, those kept in a warm room hatching first although laid last. The caterpillars emerged. at intervals until July 16. The "horns" of the newly hatched larvae were almost as long as their bodies and black in colour, giving to the tiny creatures the appearance of thorns.

One summer I startled a blackbird into dropping a large, green, white-stippled caterpillar, which proved to be that of an Eyed Hawk, *Smerinthus ocellatus* (43, 45). It was frightened but not hurt and pupated successfully and I still have its beautiful eyed moth.

The caterpillar of *Laothoe populi*, the Poplar Hawk (44), wears the family horn and has a rough skin of a pale green colour, obliquely striped with yellow. I have found it in August and September on the Black Poplar, chiefly on the succulent young shoots that surround the parent stem. It does not burrow as deeply as the Privet Hawk. The olive-grey moth rests on the bark of poplar-trees whose mossy surface it simulates; the rust-red patches on its underwings might pass for a patch of brilliant lichen. The Lime Hawk's, *Mimas tiliae* (46), greenish-yellow wings and body resemble a bunch of young leaves of the lime-tree which provides food for the caterpillar.

A year or two ago, our local chemist found among the soap and cough cures on the counter of his shop, a strange monster—snake-like in form and movements, its skin wrinkled and grey as that of an elephant; at its front end two great glaring black eyes. The chemist, having an eye for natural objects, recognised the creature as the harmless caterpillar of the Large Elephant Hawk,[1] *Deilephila elpenor*, and sent it on to me. The poor thing was glad of some rubble and moss, among which it promptly pupated inside a flimsy network cocoon. In its search for a suitable place it must have walked some distance, for the shop is backed by a yard and fronted by the street. Perhaps it had wandered from a clump of bedstraw or of willow-herb in some weedy back garden.

The caterpillar assumes this ferocious aspect in order to intimidate its enemies, and the glaring eyes are, of course, part of the hoax, being merely patches of colour. The creature's real eyes are in their proper place—on its head. This disguise is an odd prelude to the vivid beauty of the moth, whose pointed wings and body are striped with velvety rose colour and green. You will see it in the summer dusk, hovering over the honey-suckle with wing-beats so rapid as to be invisible, so that it appears to hang motionless, while with its long delicate tongue it probes the nectaries of the flowers. It appears to be guided by colour, for it has been seen hovering over artificial flowers in women's hats, and also over geraniums, which give no nectar. At twilight, too, appears the very similar Small Elephant Hawk, *Deilephila porcellus* (42), and sometimes at dusk, but usually in bright sunshine, and occasionally even in the pouring rain, you will see, darting from flower to flower of the buddleia, or the jasmine, a smaller, dun-coloured Hawk-moth with a square body and orange under-wings—the Humming-bird Hawk, *Macroglossum stellatarum* (48). One of these moths was timed and was seen to visit 194 flowers in seven minutes.

The Humming-bird is one of the migrant hawks, arriving here in varying

[1] In France these caterpillars are called "Chenilles cochonnes".

46 Two Lime Hawk-moths, *Mimas tiliae*

[Life-size]

47 Eggs of Lime Hawk-moth, *Mimas tiliae*
COLOUR: DULL GREEN WITH BROWN TINGE

[Magnification × 15]

48 Humming-Bird Hawk-moth, *Macroglossum stellatarum*, feeding
from Phlox

[*Magnification* × 1½

numbers every summer from the Continent but apparently never surviving the winter in the pupal state, although it produces two broods of brownish, white-dotted caterpillars, which feed on the bedstraw.

Our two Bee Hawk-moths, *Hemaris fuciformeis* and *Hemaris tityus*, with their flat, fluffy bodies and transparent wings, look like a cross between a Humming-bird hawk and a bumble bee. They dart about in the spring sunshine, in gardens and in wild flowery places. I have watched both species feeding from flowers of the bugle in woodland glades. The caterpillar of the Broad-bordered Bee Hawk feeds on the honeysuckle and is easy to find, as it eats small round holes in the leaf, which looks as if it had been perforated with gun-shot. Wild scabious is the food plant of the other, Narrow-bordered Bee Hawk.

The imagination is stirred by the aspect of our largest moth, the Death's Head Hawk, and by its mighty name of *Acherontia atropos* (49, 50). Fate, the relentless one, has set on its back her seal—the skull. Its upper wings are streaked with the eddies of Acheron's dark waters; the lower wings are blackened and yellow as barren sands lapped by the tides of that sad river. This vagrant from the land of shades flies when the night is at its darkest. When disturbed from its daytime rest, it utters a shrill squeak, which is caused by air being forced through its proboscis.

Although its aspect is solemn, the Death's Head is not at all a mournful moth. On the contrary, it probably enjoys itself very much in its insect way. We know it to be so fond of honey that it sometimes forces its way into a beehive with intent to rob. This trait gives it the old name of the "Bee Tiger". It is said that the squeak deceives the bees, who mistake it for the sound of their queen. Unlike most of the Hawk-moths, the Death's Head has a short, strong proboscis, with which it breaks through the wax covers of the honey-cells and feasts at leisure. The bees sometimes set on the intruder and sting it to death and build round it a mausoleum of wax, to prevent it from fouling the hive.

The Death's Head[1] is a migrant from the Continent to the south and west of England, and, less frequently, to other counties too, where it leaves offspring in the shape of enormous purple-striped brown and green caterpillars that are occasionally found in potato fields (the country people used to call them "tatur-dorgs") or in gardens, or rarely, on the leaves of the tea-tree. One such was recently discovered by the gardener of some neighbours in Wiltshire, who gave it to me; but it had been put, when about to pupate, into a soft-sided box of earth, which caved in, and the unfortunate occupant perished at the critical moment of metamorphosis.

The caterpillar burrows in the autumn and constructs a large underground cell, and the pupa usually remains in this subterranean chamber for a year, sometimes for as much as eighteen months, emerging in the month

---

[1] In am told that in Egypt, where it is common, this moth is called "the Father of the Village".

of May. More often it appears as a perfect insect in October. It has a
habit of coming into houses in wet weather during late autumn. One of
my earliest and most vivid recollections is of being taken as a small child
to the house of a neighbour, to see the giant moth which had thus taken
refuge. It seemed as large as a bird (the wings measure from $4\frac{1}{2}$ inches to
5 inches when expanded) and their sombre colouring of black and brown
and ochre bore an indescribably beautiful purple bloom, which disappears
when the moth is dead. How I longed, but in vain, to have the wonderful
creature for my very own. (It was given to a grown-up entomologist; so
you see that what with this disappointment and the other mishap, I
have had no luck in my quest for the Death's Head Hawk.)

Life being what it is—a series of substitutions—I have had to content
myself with the lesser thrill of finding, on the wooden door of a hen-house,
a sleeping Convolvulus Hawk, *Herse convolvuli*. Its pointed grey upper
wings have almost as great a span as those of the Death's Head. This is
one of the most powerful and swiftest of Hawk-moths; it shoots through
the air like a projectile. It visits us erratically in June and July from
Germany and the south of France and its caterpillars have been found in
Britain, feeding on the convolvulus.

But the Convolvulus Hawk is chiefly remarkable for its tongue, which
is four inches long, and with which it feeds from the tubular flowers of
its favourite, the tobacco. During the pupal stage this proboscis is encased
in a tube which projects from the head in a loop, like the handle of a jug.
This extraordinary tongue, from which the moth derived its old name of
Unicorn Hawk, gave rise also to a superstition, current among country
people, that the moth stings with its tongue.

I have never met with our native Pine Hawk, *Hycloicus pinastri*, whose
chief haunts are in Suffolk, Dorset and Hants. As its name suggests, its
caterpillars feed on needles of the pine, on the trunk of which the brownish
moth sleeps by day, disguised as a knot in the bark. This insect is, I
believe, very common at times on the Continent, where the caterpillars do
great damage to pine woods. Our other migrant Hawk-moths, are all
Continental insects, very rare in Britain. But there are surprises in store
for all of us, and perhaps you will be as fortunate as I was when, on a June
morning in 1943, I found on my doorstep a match-box and inside it, in
perfect condition, a living male striped Hawk-moth, *Celerio livornica*.
Our local roadman had found it early that morning, concealed among
the roadside grasses. This moth was a member of an immigration of
several hundreds of these superb creatures that spread over the south of
England during a summer memorable for other migrants also. Or, when
you are wandering among sand-dunes by the sea, it is not impossible that
you may find, feeding on the sea-spurge, the caterpillars of the Spurge Hawk,
Celerio euphorbiae. The Bedstraw Hawk, *Celerio galii*, normally rare, is very
occasionally widespread throughout Britain. In July 1934, it went as
far north as Uist in the Shetland Isles.

49   Earthen Cocoon and Chrysalis of Death's-head Hawk-moth
Acherontia atropos   [*Life-size*

50   Death's-head Hawk-moth, *Acherontia atropos*
[*Magnification* × 1½

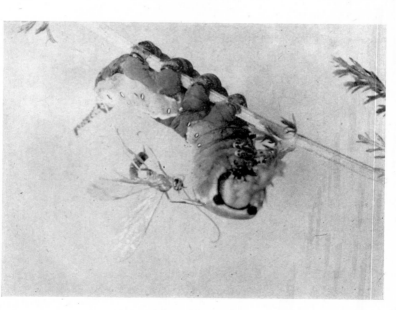

51   Ichneumon Fly attacking Puss Moth (*Cerura vinula*) Caterpillar

[*Enlarged*

52   Puss Moths, *Cerura vinula*

[*Smaller than life*

These four moths are rather alike in appearance. All are variously striped and streaked with olive, palest yellow and silvery white and their underwings are flushed with rose. But you cannot mistake that greatest rarity of all, the Oleander Hawk, *Deilephila nerii*, for it has an abnormally long pointed body of velvet green and its wings are adorned with a green patchwork pattern. This moth makes a long journey, for it travels from the shores of the Mediterranean. In its southern home the caterpillars feed on the Oleander, but in northern lands they content themselves with leaves of the periwinkles, on which, in Britain, they have occasionally been found.

Resting Privet Hawk-moth
Sphinx ligustri
(*Rather larger than life-size*)

CHAPTER XIII

The Prominents (Notodontidae) and Tussocks (Lymantriidae)

YOUR acquaintance with the moths of the *Notodontidae*, or Prominent family, will probably begin by your finding one or other of their caterpillars; for the moths fly at night and are rapid on the wing and are therefore rarely seen except when attracted to a bright light. There are, in Britain, about twenty-five species of this family, none of them migrants. The most striking are the Puss Moth, *Cerura vinula* (51, 52), which is generally distributed, the rather common Buff-tip, *Phalera bucephala*, and the less common Lobster, *Stauropus fagi* (54, 55).

In May you may find the smooth brown eggs of the Puss Moth in twos and threes on the upper surface of poplar and sallow leaves, where they simulate galls. The mother moth (52), seems to prefer the young saplings that grow in riverside thickets. And in July and August you may come upon the caterpillar—black when young, an inch and a half long when full-grown, portly withal and excessively odd in appearance and attitude. It clings to its twig with black-goloshed feet, by its middle claspers only, for the end pair is lacking and its body tapers to a point. Its front and hinder parts are raised like the prow and boom of a ship. Its hump-backed green form is cleverly camouflaged by a saddle of purple-brown, which breaks up its outline, so that it appears to be wrapped in two leaves. At its front end, two sham eyes, red-rimmed and baleful, frighten away the birds, while its posterior bears, inside two knobbed black sheaths, a pair of red whips, weapons of defence against its dreaded enemy the ichneumon fly (51), which fancies this particular kind of caterpillar as a larder for her loathsome progeny. Tickle the caterpillar with a grass-blade and it arches its front segments, displaying the dreadful "face"; up goes its "behind" in a curve over his back, like the tail of an angry goat, and the red whips dart forth, lashing and writhing in fury. If goaded still further, the caterpillar spurts out a deadly acid which is most painful if it gets into your eyes.

Take the caterpillar home and you can watch its habits. You will see that the terrifying "face" does not appear until its final moult. Its front end is knobbed during the earlier stages. You will notice too that it bears between the whip-sheaths a small spine, used to flick away its ejected excrement.

If you find it when full-fed, give it some bits of bark, or, when its purple colour shows that it is about to pupate, put it into a good-sized match-box. Gnawing sounds will presently indicate that the inmate is chewing it up to make a cocoon. This, when finished, is a dome-like affair, composed of bark and of glue and so hard that it is impossible to

53   Caterpillar of Pebble Prominent, *Notodonta ziczac*
[*Much enlarged*

54   Lobster Moth Caterpillar, *Stauropus fagi*
[*Rather larger than life*

55   Lobster Moth, *Stauropus fagi*

[*Magnification* × 3

cut it with a knife. If left on the tree the caterpillar fixes it to the bark where it can be found during winter. It seems that there is no gadget that this creature, in one or other of its stages, is without. The pupa's head is furnished with a cutting instrument with which, when ready to hatch, it saws at the weak end of its prison; a drop of a softening fluid,

Puss Moth, *Cerura vinula*, Caterpillars
(Life-size)

secreted by the moth, completes the process and out comes that softest, fluffiest of creatures, the Puss Moth.

And if you don't find the Puss, perhaps you will discover the rather similar, but smaller, caterpillar of one of its relatives, the Sallow Kitten, *Cerura furcula*, or the Poplar Kitten, *Cerura hermelina*. Their cocoons also are constructed on the bark of a tree. Or, in places where willows and birches grow, you may meet with the curious humped caterpillar of the Pebble Prominent, *Notodonta ziczac* (53), or of another Prominent, *Notodonta dromedarius*, whose cocoon, composed of earth and silk, lies at the foot of the tree. The moth of the Pebble Prominent can be recognised

The Pupa of the Puss Moth, *Cerura vinula*
(*Life-size*)
is armed with a cutting instrument, with which it saws away the weak end of its
cocoon. The moth ejects a drop of softening fluid which melts the wood fibres,
and emerges with part of the pupa-case on its head.

by a round patch, like a pebble, or perhaps more like a knot of wood, near the tip of its forewings. The Coxcomb Prominent has streaky buff and brown wings with a wavy edge, while the Pale Prominent's long body ends in a cleft bunch of hair. You can recognise most moths of this family by a tooth-like tuft of scales, projecting from the middle of the inner margin of the forewings. When the moth is resting these tufts are raised like a fan above the back of the closed wings.

To combat the ichneumon menace (18, 19, 51, 78), the caterpillar of the Lobster Moth (54, 55) has devised an effectual weapon. It ejects in the face of its enemy a spray of formic acid which is death to the fly and would, I think, blind the eyes of a bird. This caterpillar certainly looks capable of anything. It is a most evil-looking object, humped, wrinkled, with long waving forelegs resembling those of the crustacean whose name it bears.

The Buff-tip, *Phalera bucephala*, is a distant relation only of the true Prominents, and its

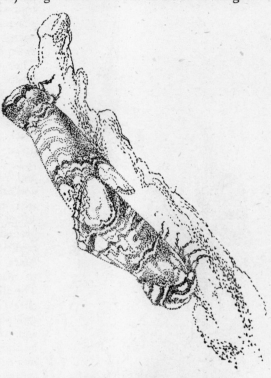

A Pair of Buff-tips, *Phalera bucephala*
(*Slightly larger than life*)

caterpillar (57), is not humped as theirs are. It has no weapons, but its yellow and black stripes proclaim the fact that it is distasteful and the birds heed the warning and keep at a distance. It is very ugly—a mean sort of creature—and gregarious when young, and seemingly omnivorous in a mild vegetarian way, for it will eat the foliage of almost any tree. Sometimes, in a lime avenue, or a plantation of hazels, you will see the branches stripped by these caterpillars. They fall off when full-fed and crawl about everywhere, looking for soft ground in which they burrow and lie, as reddish-brown pupae, unprotected by any cocoon, throughout the winter. When resting with its buff-tipped wings wrapped round its body, the moth is so absurdly like a broken stick that it is easily overlooked.

The caterpillars of the *Lymantriidae*, or Tussock family, flaunting their "warning colours" on bush and hedgerow, will also attract your attention and compel your admiration, for their multi-coloured stripes and tufts are most ornamental. The family badge is a row of flat-topped tufts, like miniature shaving brushes, worn along the back, with side-tufts, and a sweeping plume on the tail. The most beautiful of these creatures is the Pale Tussock, or Hop Dog, a vision of palest green and white silky fur, banded on the body with velvet black. Its brushes are lemon-green and his tail-plume rose-red. It feeds by night in July and August on the hop, elm and oak, on the leaves of which it rests during the day. Its silken cocoon is spun above ground in odd corners and the resulting moth, *Dasychira pudibunda*, which varies somewhat in its markings, emerges in June. The allied Dark Tussock, *Dasychira fascelina* (56), has a black caterpillar tufted with yellow and white which feeds on the heather and the broom and rolls in a ring when disturbed. It is commonest in the north of England.

Pale Tussock Moth, *Dasychira pudibunda*,
Males, and Cocoon
(*Life-size*)

In June you will often see the caterpillars of the Yellow-tail, *Euproctis similis* (p. 76), arrogantly gay in scarlet, black and white, decorating the branches of apple trees and of hawthorns. These creatures bear on their backs odd little glands, or warts; their function may be to secrete a drop of fluid noxious to their enemies. Or are they, perhaps, an apparatus for registering atmospheric conditions, such as J. H. Fabre observed on the backs of caterpillars of the Pine Processionary? [1] The caterpillar of the

---

[1] See *The Life of the Caterpillar*, Chapter IV, by J. H. Fabre.

57 Young Buff-tip Caterpillars, *Phalera bucephala*

[*About life-size*

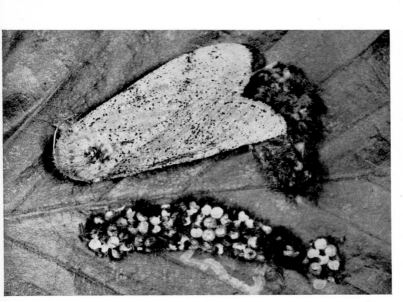

56 A Female Dark Tussock Moth, *Dasychira fascelina*,
covering her eggs with fluff from her body

[*Magnification* × 2½

60   Eggs of Silver Cloud Moth
Xylomiges conspicillaris
COLOUR: PALE GREY, FINELY RIBBED

[*Magnification* × 35]

59   Eggs of Fox Moth
Macrothylacia rubi
COLOUR: BROWNISH WHITE WITH BROWN RINGS

[*Magnification* × 20]

58   Eggs of Pale Prominent Moth
Pterostoma palpina
COLOUR: PALE GREENISH WHITE

[*Magnification* × 35]

allied, less common, Brown-tail, *Euproctis chrysorrhaea*, has the same odd warts. Its black body is striped on each side with red and adorned with brown hairs and white side tufts.

Hop Dog (Pale Tussock), *Dasychira pudibunda*, Caterpillars on Hop
(*Life-size*)

No birds will touch these caterpillars, except the cuckoo, which has been known to gorge on them to the extent of implanting a coat of bristling hairs in its gizzard. The hairs "moult" easily and stick in a bird's throat, and also bring out a painful rash on the human skin.

J. H. Fabre examined the irritant hairs of caterpillars and found that they are in themselves harmless, and that their virulence is caused by a coating of poisonous matter. He removed this virus by means of a solvent, reduced it by evaporation, soaked a pad in the liquid and tied it to his arm. In a few hours the poison took effect, and produced a running sore, accompanied by burning pains and itching that endured for five days. Suspecting that this poison was a waste product thrown off by the caterpillar, Fabre than made further experiments with the blood of the caterpillar and with the droppings of silkworms and of various other caterpillars, of

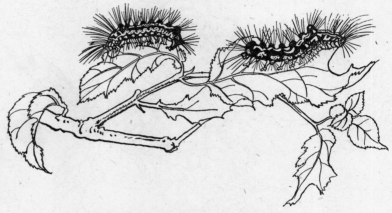

Yellow-tail Caterpillars, *Euproctis similis*
(*Life-size*)

moths and butterflies. He tested also the drops of liquid ejected by butterflies and moths at the moment of their emergence. All were found to possess the same irritant quality. He thus came to the conclusion that all caterpillars are to a certain extent poisonous and that their virus is an off-throw of their metabolism, a digestive residue; gregarious caterpillars being the most poisonous, from the fact that their hairs are in constant contact with the droppings that foul the interior of their web.

But to return to our Tussocks. The Yellow-tail spins a silken cocoon, and the moth is, save for its yellow tail, purest white in hue and rests amid foliage like a snowflake out of season.

They are motherly creatures, these Tussocks. The female Yellow-tail carries at the end of her abdomen a pair of pincers, with which she tweaks down off her body and spreads it over her new-laid eggs. You may watch her combing the down, spreading it evenly, and finally giving the finishing touches to the silky coverlet, exactly like a human mother tucking up her baby. The Brown-tail also provides a blanket for her eggs, and stays near them to see that they are safe. The Dark Tussock (56), takes the same care of her offspring, while the female of the Vapourer, *Orgyia antiqua*, is

PLATE VIII.

Top left: BURNISHED BRASS. *Top left (just below):* GREY DAGGER. *Lower left centre:* SILVER Y (ON STALK). *Below on left:* GARDEN TIGER. *Bottom left:* YELLOW UNDERWING. *Top right:* RED UNDERWING. *Lower right:* CREAM-SPOT TIGER *Bottom right:* FEATHERED GOTHIC.

the most domesticated of them all. She overdoes things rather, in her maternal zeal; all is sacrificed for the sake of the children. She leads a dull life, this poor mother; no outings, not a drop of nectar. When the other moths flaunt their finery at the banquet of the flowers, she alone is absent. And what a fright she is! She has not even any wings; she is just an inert grey bag of a body, with two little flippers where her wings ought to be and she spends her whole life at home, clinging to the outside of her pupal cocoon, on the surface of which she proceeds to lay four or five hundred eggs. Then, her mission in life fulfilled, she dies; and her hand-some-winged spouse, seeking, perhaps, a little distraction after the dullness of home, continues to dither about in the sunshine. You will recognise him by his chestnut-coloured wings with their one white spot, and by his fringed antennæ, and you may meet him in gardens, in country lanes and also in Kensington High Street and in Piccadilly, where the London limes provide food for his handsome red-brown, tufted caterpillars.

Moths of this family, when resting with folded wings, are very much like feathers. You might easily mistake the Yellow-tail and the Brown-tail for white hen's feathers, caught up in the tree. The Dark (56), and Pale Tussocks are mottled like the feathers of a partridge and rest with their forelegs stretched out in front of them like the quill of the feather, and their fluffiness completes the illusion. The Black Arches, *Lymantria monacha*, has a zigzag pattern of black on white, like the feathers of a guinea-fowl. When resting on the bark of a tree, as is its habit, this "disruptive" colouring has the effect of breaking up the moth's outline, so that it is nearly invisible. But whiter and more shining than any swan's feather are the lovely wings of the White Satin Moth, *Leucoma salicis*, which, though a resident here, like the rest of its family, is something of a traveller too; for it has been seen arriving in swarms on the East Coast and there is also a record of a mass flight in Germany.

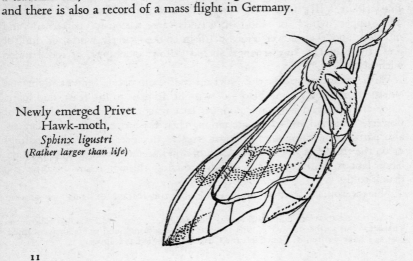

Newly emerged Privet
Hawk-moth,
Sphinx ligustri
(*Rather larger than life*)

CHAPTER XIV

The Noctuids (Noctuidae)[1]

WHEN the sun sets, the flowers of day close their petals. Their visitors, the bees and butterflies, are already asleep. Now, with the deepening dusk, the flowers of night open and exhale their fragrance. Night-scented stock, tobacco, evening primrose and white starry jasmine send forth a summons to their guests, the moths.

If you take your lantern into the garden, you can witness the dance of these creatures of the night. The darkness is full of their coming and going. Evanescent shapes weave in and out of the trees. A Ghost Moth droops its white plumes in the grass, too feeble of flight to reach the banquet spread above. Nebulous wings whirr round the flowers; a big moth alights on the petals with a flop. A shape like an aerial torpedo shoots past, hangs for a moment over a flower and is gone. Slender-bodied Geometers zigzag hither and thither; thick-bodied moths buzz round your lantern and sink, dazed, into the grass.

These thick-set moths of various sizes, dappled and dun, dusky and grey, belong to the numerous company of the Noctuids. You may arouse them from their daytime slumbers when you are gardening, or picking flowers. When thus disturbed, they scuttle away through the undergrowth like mice. They are also to be found by day reposing on walls, or on tree-trunks. Some of them—the Dark Arches (61), for instance, and the Yellow Underwing (Plate VIII), rest with their wings laid flat, the upper pair completely covering the lower, Others, such as the Burnished Brass (Plate VIII), fold their wings in the shape of a steep-pitched roof. The upper wings of most Noctuids are variously patterned and mottled, and their lower wings plain in colour—pearly white, or dun, or grey; those of the "underwings" being yellow, or orange, or red, banded with black.

With some exceptions, the Noctuid moths are active only at night and emerge from their hiding-places as twilight deepens to fly, feast, and mate. They are equipped with long tongues that reach deep into the chalices of flowers. Valerian and phlox are among their favourite plants and they are also partial to a compound of sugar, treacle and beer, smeared on palings or on the trunks of trees, with a dash of amyl-acetate to scent the night air. Your lantern will reveal the greedy, jostling throng; many become too drunk to fly.

The caterpillars feed by night either on the foliage of trees, or among

---

[1] According to scientific classification, the Lackeys, Eggars and Footmen follow the Tussocks; but as the manner of this book is conversational, and as its shape seemed best as I have written it, I have left the Chapters arranged as follows.

61 Dark Arches, *Apamea monoglypha*, resting on Birch trunk

[*Magnification* × 2

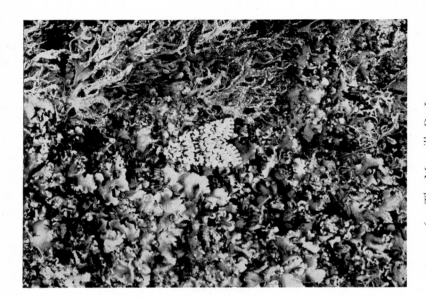

63 The Merveille Du Jour
    Griposia aprilina
    Showing its protective coloration

62 Caterpillar of the Merveille Du Jour
    Griposia aprilina
    It feeds at night on oak leaves

the low-growing plants of field and hedgerow. Sometimes they devour the precious plants in your garden, and it is very difficult to find the marauders, which hide most cunningly by day, usually in dead leaves and rubble at the roots of their food-plants. The majority of them do not hibernate as caterpillars but pupate in the autumn in a rough cocoon of earth and leaves glued together, or in a spun cocoon, or sometimes in a chink of bark or under the earth with no cocoon at all. But there are many species of Noctuid that hibernate as caterpillars and there are some that sleep through the winter as moths.

They are at first sight rather a drab company, these Noctuids. There are so many different kinds, and many of the species are so much alike. One becomes lost in a maze of Clays and Rustics, of Darts and Under-wings (Plate VIII), and Wainscots. To confuse you further, moths of the same species are often exceedingly variable.

Then, too, the rather clumsy shape of the commoner Noctuids does not lend itself to display when set in the moth cabinet. There are exceptions; the Herald is decorative and so is the Burnished Brass (Plate VIII)—but if looked at attentively, these humble moths are seen to lack neither richness nor originality and there are, among their numerous assemblage, some real beauties—the Angle Shades (Plate IX), the Old Lady, and the Red Underwing (Plate VIII). Some of the smaller moths, also, are charming in their mottled simulation of mosses and lichen. You must see them in their natural surroundings—small furry creatures, crouching among the leaves and lichen that blend with their mealy wings in a harmony of browns and greens and greys.

These moths, with their sober raiment and jackets of brown fur, take on a different aspect when viewed under a lens. Our unaided human sight permits us to see them only as small insects. Were we gifted with a different vision, they would appear to us as creatures of the size of cats, or owls; while the larger moths would be as imposing as leopards. The structure of the moths, although so different, is as perfect as that of the larger vertebrate animals, and their detail is even more exquisite.

The Dark Arches, *Apamea monoglypha* (61), is a very variable moth and ranges from greyish fawn through brown to black. The Light Arches, *Apamea lithoxylea*, on the other hand, varies little. It is a common and a nondescript-looking insect, like a wisp of dry grass. Prettier are its allies, the Grey Arches, *Polia nebulosa*, and the Silvery Arches, *Polia tincta*, both of them beautifully mottled with grey; while the Green Arches, *Anaplectoides prasina* is at its best when freshly emerged, for its green ground-colour soon fades to an ochreous brown.

These Noctuid "Arches" must not be confused with the Black Arches, which is, as we have seen, a member of the Tussock family.

Green moths are unusual: there is among the Noctuids, a beauty, the Merveille de jour, *Griposia aprilina* (62, 63). It frequents woods, where the insect appears in September. The eggs remain dormant through the winter, and the caterpillar (62), feeds from April to June on oak leaves and then pupates deep in the earth.

The caterpillar of this early moth is difficult to rear. The eggs, if found, must be kept on ice, or they will hatch before the young leaves have burgeoned.

A smaller Noctuid, the Campion, *Hadena cucubali*, shows a pattern as of pale lace spread over the dark brown velvet of its wings. It flies in June and there is a partial second generation in August. Its caterpillar eats into the leaves and the unripe seed of the bladder campion. This "lace" pattern has thickened and become blurred in the smaller wings of the Tawny Shears, *Hadena lepida*. Its relation, the pretty little Broad-barred White, *Hadena serena*, is quite different in appearance. It has a protective colouring of chalky white, banded and mottled with grey, which enables it to rest undetected upon walls and rocks.

In the Feathered Gothic, *Tholera popularia* (Plate VIII), and the Gothic, *Phalaena typica*, the "lace" pattern appears again and more distinctively, as the meshes of a pale golden net veiling the glossy dark wings. The Feathered Gothic has plumed antennæ, and the Antler, *Cerapteryx graminis* derives its name from a similar feature. Its caterpillars are, as I said before, a pest on grasslands and sometimes lay waste acres of pasture.

The "Clays" and the "Rustics" can be recognised by their ground-colour of pinkish ochre or warm umber, which is variously streaked and shaded and, in most species, stamped with small distinctive dark marks. These give their names to the Triple-spotted Clay, *Amathes ditrapezium*, the Double Square-spot, *Amathes triangulum*, and the Setaceous Hebrew Character, *Amathes c-nigrum*. Three spots distinguish the Autumnal Rustic, *Amathes glareosa*, while the markings of the Double Dart, *Graphiphora augur*, are like a scrawl of hieroglyphics. Moths of this group are liable to aberration, the Engrailed Clay being a particularly variable species.

You will know the "Darts" by their "hall-marks" stamped on wings of a dark and dusky brown, and described by their names of Shuttle-shaped Dart, Heart and Dart, and Heart and Club.

Their relative, the Turnip Moth, *Agrotis segetum*, lacks distinctive markings and is a broken brown in colour with underwings of pearly white. Though uninteresting in appearance, it has a claim to notoriety, for the caterpillar is a pest in fields, where it eats large cavities in the roots of turnips and swedes.

The Noctuas are divided into thirteen sub-families, of which one, the *Acronyctinae*, has hairy caterpillars, some of them as decorative as those of the Tussocks. That of the Sycamore Moth, *Apatele aceris*, is clothed with a mane of bright yellow hairs, varied by tufts of red and by a row of black spots along the back. I have found it in London—although discovered beneath a horse-chestnut tree, it would eat nothing but beech leaves and slept during the day curled up on the underside of a leaf. Its cocoon was of silk, mixed with hairs, spun in a corner of my cage. The moth, which

Top left—Grey Dagger, *Apatele psi*
Lower Centre—Yellow Underwing, *Triphaena pronuba*
Centre—Broad-bordered Yellow Underwing, *Lampra fimbria*
Top right—Silver Y, *Plusia gamma*
Bottom right—Double Dart, *Graphiphora augur*
            (*Life-size*)

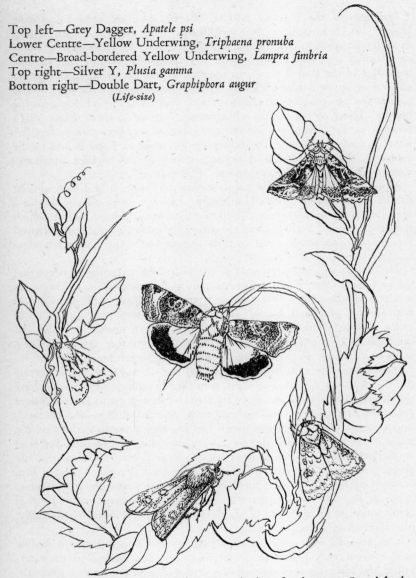

appears in June, is mottled with various shades of pale grey. It might be
mistaken for its near ally, the Poplar Grey, *Apatele megacephala* (64), which
is, actually, darker in colour. The rather similar Dark Dagger, *Apatele
tridens*, and Grey Dagger, *Apatele psi* (Plate VIII), wear a "badge" of four
black daggers on each upper wing.

The eggs of the Noctuid Moths (66, 67, 68), are shaped like tiny lobster-pots, beautifully ribbed and fluted. The shape and pattern vary in different species, that of the Brindled Green, *Drybotodes protea*, has a resemblance to a closed flower bud. Its upright converging ribs are like the edges of the folded petals; in the spaces between them, short pointed ribs curve upwards like enclosing sepals. You may find the eggs of the commoner Noctuids fastened to grasses and to leaves of low-growing plants. Those of the Yellow Underwing, *Triphaena pronuba* (Plate VIII), conform to the lobster-pot pattern and produce ugly brownish caterpillars which are often a pest in the flower garden, both in London and in the country. The moth's habit of hiding indoors, behind curtains and book-shelves, gives it the German name of "Hausmutter".

Almost as common as the Large Yellow Underwing, and with similar habits, is the Lesser Yellow Underwing, *Triphaena comes*. There is also a very handsome Broad-bordered Yellow Underwing, *Lampra fimbria*, which frequents woods. You will find the rather common Lesser Broad-bordered Underwing, *Triphaena janthina*, in fields and gardens. All three moths come to a light.

The largest and most splendid of the Noctuids is the Red Underwing, *Catocala nupta* (Plate VIII), which rests on palings and walls and hides its scarlet and black lower wings with a grey upper pair, scribbled all over with darker grey and black. It is common everywhere, especially in valleys favourable to the willow and poplar, which provide food for the caterpillar. I have found the moth in Suffolk, resting on the wooden walls of a cottage, and also on the trunks of the Scotch pine.

I must mention the Wainscots, which are, in appearance, excessively dull. There is a sameness in their unmarked, unmottled wings that have the colour of dead grass or of winter reeds. No doubt this is an excellent protection, for they live among reed-beds, and in saltings, and on sand-dunes by the sea. The female moth lays her eggs in small bathces on the stalks of reeds and grasses and the caterpillars bore into the stem and feed on the inner pith. As the stem is hollow, there is plenty of room for the growing occupant, which eats through the reed, leaving a flimsy film between itself and the outer air. When the time comes for it to pupate, it is just the right size to fit into the hollow of the reed, without either being squeezed or in danger of slipping and the pupa lodges comfortably, like a kernel in a nut.

It is provided with little hooks, which enable it to move up the hollow reed. When ready to emerge, it climbs to the exit gnawed by the cater-pillar, and forces its way through the thin wall, and the moth crawls out, leaving its empty shell sticking in the breach.

The caterpillar in its stronghold is, nevertheless, not secure from enemies. The ichneumon fly thrusts her long ovipositor into its body through the thin film of the reed. And birds are on the look-out, too. A naturalist once watched a moorhen hunting for wainscot caterpillars. She went

64 Caterpillar of Poplar Grey Moth, *Apatele megacephala*
[*Life-size*

65 Caterpillar of Angle Shades Moth, *Phlogophora meticulosa*
[*About twice life-size*

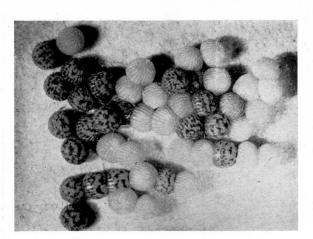

68 Eggs of Early Grey Moth
Xylōcampa areola
A noctuid moth which may be found in March and
April in the daytime, resting on posts and tree-trunks.
The caterpillar feeds at night on honeysuckle
COLOUR: IMMATURE, WHITE; DEVELOPING,
DULL WHITE, MARKED ROSY RED
[*Magnification* × 15]

67 Eggs of Feathered Gothic
Moth
Tholera popularia
COLOUR: PEARLY CREAM
[*Magnification* × 20]

66 Eggs of Sweet Gale Moth
Apatele euphorbiae var. myricae
COLOUR: PALE WHITISH YELLOW,
BLOTCHED BLOOD RED
[*Magnification* × 25]

to work methodically, tapping the reeds with her beak. Where they rang hollow she went on her way; but when the muffled sound showed that the stem was tenanted, she made a jab and brought out the caterpillar in her beak.

There is a Common Wainscot, *Leucania pallens*, which feeds on grasses, a Shore Wainscot, *Leucania littorali*, which thrives on the marram grass, a Bullrush Wainscot, *Nonagria typhae*, and many others—about twenty all told, of this curious company.

Let us now turn to brighter wings and to caterpillars less secluded in their habits.

The sand-dunes and the blue sea beyond them, evoke distant lands and far journeyings; and we call to mind once more the periodical wanderings of the moths. Of the Noctuids, a dozen and more are migrants, some being regular visitors to Britain, others rare stragglers. We have the American Wainscot, *Leucania unipuncta*, the Delicate, *Leucania vitellina*, the Dark Sword-grass, *Agrotis ipsilon*, and the Pearly Underwing, *Agrotis aucia*; the Bordered Straw, *Heliothis peltigera*, the Scarce Bordered Straw, *Heliothis armigera*, and others. Several of them are pests in other countries. The Scarce Bordered Straw is the "American Boil-worm" of cotton, and the Mottled Willow is known as the "Beet Army Worm" in the U.S.A., and is, also, a pest in South Africa. The Dark-Sword grass is destructive to wheat in Egypt, where it goes by the name of the "Greasy Cut-worm."

But our most regular Noctuid migrant is the Silver Y, *Plusia gamma* (Plate VIII), which comes from the Continent, sometimes in swarms, every summer. This moth compels our interest and arouses our curiosity by its habit of migrating at the same time, and to the same destination, as the Painted Lady butterfly and the Rush Veneer, a small brown moth of a different family. Why these three travellers should combine is a puzzle to entomologists. Their food-plants are different and their habits have, as a rule, nothing in common.

The Silver Y migrants arrive on these shores at the same time as the Painted Lady, namely, in late May or early June, and lay eggs on various low plants, and the second generation of the moth appears in August. It flies by day and is common throughout England, especially in the south and west, on heathery lands. It is purplish brown, like old brocade, the upper wings marked with its insignia, the Y, or Greek Gamma, of silver. Prettier still is its relation, the Beautiful Golden Y, *Plusia pulchrina*, clad in a more sumptuous brocade of rose and brown, threaded with gold and bearing on each wing two central golden spots. An allied species, *Plusia moneta*, formerly a rare migrant, evidently found our country to its liking, for it increased in numbers and finally settled down here as a native of Britain. Its caterpillars thrive on the delphinium in our gardens, where the moth is not uncommonly to be found.

The homely stinging-nettle provides food for the green caterpillars of another moth of the same genus, *Plusia chrysitis*, the Burnished Brass

(Plate VIII). Unlike most of the Noctuids, this caterpillar hibernates
through the winter and becomes full-fed in May and the moth makes a
glorious appearance in July and August. It has wings of a shining beaten
gold which changes in some lights, to a metallic green. A diagonal streak
of brown runs across them and matches the fur of the body, which is
arranged in a collar, with two fan-like tippets spread over the back.

There is one Noctuid caterpillar that is conspicuous during the daytime in July and August, namely, that of the Mullein Shark, *Cucullia
verbasci*. It is "eau-de-nil" in colour, banded with yellow and dotted with
black, and it rests on the upper sides of mullein leaves, where large holes

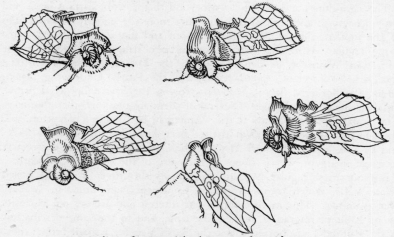

Studies of a Burnished Brass, *Plusia chrysitis*
(Rather larger than life)

and a trail of droppings betray its presence. This caterpillar pupates
underground in a tough cocoon of earth, and the moth which emerges
during the following May or June is one of the few Noctuids with a pure
and beautiful line. Its narrow curved wings appear as if fashioned from some
precious wood, varied, near the margins, with an inlay of a darker colour.

Rather similar in shape and size, but less beautiful, is the Shark,
Cucullia umbratica, which may be compared to a rough shaving discarded
from the wood of the other.

Mormo maura, the Old Lady, is well described by her name. She is a
large and portly moth with voluminous wings of rusty black, edged with a
frill. When seen through a lens, she appears as the great-grandmother
of all the goblins. She trails robes of a sombre brocaded velvet, sparsely
threaded with gold; her shoulders are hunched under a great fur collar,
and a witch's face peers from a hood of fur. There are spines on the
creature's spindly shanks. She flies into our houses by night and creeps
behind curtains; but you need not fear her—she is a benevolent sprite.

PLATE IX.

Top left: SPECKLED YELLOW.   *Top right:* LATTICED HEATH.   *Centre:*
SWALLOWTAILED-MOTH.   *Lower left:* ANGLE SHADES.   *Lower right:* WAVED
UMBER.   *Bottom Centre:* TREBLE-BAR.

I will end my notes on these moths with a mention of two favourites. One, the Herald, *Scoliopteryx libatrix*, hibernates as a perfect insect. It appears in June and a second generation emerges in September and October and can then be found feasting on the blossoms of the ivy, and soon after-

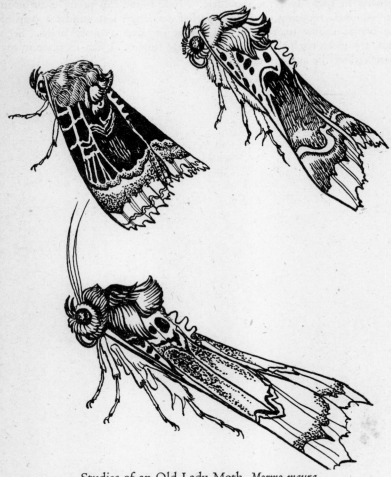

Studies of an Old Lady Moth, *Mormo maura*
(*Larger than life*)

wards it seeks out suitable winter quarters in a shed, outhouse or belfry. It is then that you find it indoors. Its protective colouring is original, for it stimulates a lump of rust: legs, crested body, and indented upper wings are plumed with brown and reddish scales of a texture most exquisite.

Another, that delights me anew every time that I find it, is the Angle Shades, *Phlogophora meticulosa* (Plate IX). The living moth pleases as much by its mealy texture as by the creamy yellow of its body and wings that are flushed with pinkish brown and marked by a border and two inner triangles, of olive green. There is also a triangle, and two yellow fur tippets, on the back. When at rest, the wings are slightly crumpled and the antennæ lie back along the shoulders. I have found this pretty creature in late summer, reposing on a dew-pearled dandelion leaf amidst a crop of the brittle yellow toad-stools that sprout up after a misty night. Seen thus, the moth itself is not unlike a strange fungus. It has its place in my memories of the autumn days.

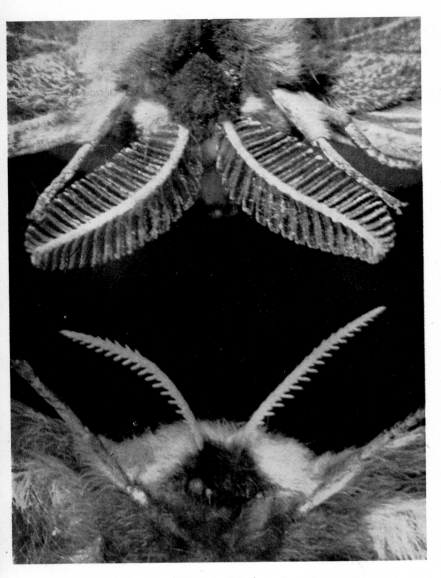

69   Antennæ of Emperor Moths,   *Saturnia pavonia*

Above–Male   *Below*–Female

[*Highly magnified*

71 Kentish Glory Moth, *Endromis versicolora*

70 Emperor Moth, *Saturnia pavonia*, just emerged with wings
stretched over back, drying

The Emperor (Saturniidae), the Eggars (Lasiocampidae), Tigers (Arctiinae) and Footmen (Lithosiinae)

THE sensory equipment of moths is adapted to a nocturnal existence. Their eyes are bigger than those of the butterflies, and the lenses are receptive to rays of subdued light, and, probably, sensitive also to rays unperceived by the human retina.

Although a few moths of dusk seem to be guided by sight, most of the night-flying species rely chiefly on their sense of smell, and their organs of smell, the antennæ, are accordingly highly developed. Their shape is visible to a certain extent to the naked eye. When viewed under a lens a curious diversity of structure is apparent. Some are seen to be composed of a number of simple joints, welded together in the form of a thread. In some species the sex can be ascertained by the larger size of the joint nearest the head. In many moths the joints are toothed; in others, each "tooth" bears a hair, or a tuft of hairs. Some are formed of a chain of angular plates. But the most striking form is that of a stem, or shaft, fringed on one or both sides with long fine hairs, each of these lateral rays sometimes being fringed also. This gives to the antennæ the appearance of beautiful plumes, like ostrich feathers. The plume-like form appears in male moths only of several species, and is associated with an extraordinary power of sensing, and finding, the female moth from a distance. This is known as "assembling".

It is a faculty possessed, to a certain extent, by many species among which may be mentioned some moths of the Geometer family: the Mottled Umber, the Pale Brindled Beauty, the Scarce Umber, and the Winter Moth, of which the females are all wingless. But it is most marked in moths of other families: the Kentish Glory (71), the Emperor (Plate X and 69, 70), and the Oak Eggar (72) and Fox Moth.

The female moths of "assembling" species are big-bodied, lethargic creatures with slender antennæ. Even the winged females do not fly far and might be overlooked by suitors—for both sexes are short-lived, and their time for mating lasts for a few days only—were it not for the "assembling" faculty, which is possessed by both sexes. The mature female is endowed with the property of distilling a mysterious alembic, imperceptible to our senses, which radiates to a considerable distance, informing male moths of her presence. A nubile female will attract a concourse of suitors, who come to her from all points of the compass, sometimes from a distance of four kilometres, both up and down wind. The love-philtre is effective even when the female is imprisoned in a closed, but ventilated, box.

This phenomenon has been exhaustively studied by scientists, who have experimented in various ways in order to ascertain the nature of the emanation, which operates effectively even when a captive female is surrounded by the strongest of chemical and vegetable smells. The emanation apparently saturates any object with which the moth's body remains in contact: an empty box, for example, in which a female has been imprisoned, retains traces of the effluvia and will attract males for some time afterwards.

The female stores this substance, or scent, in organs placed in her skin, usually between the eighth and ninth abdominal segments. If the scent-organs are cut out, and laid near the female, the male moth will alight on the excised organs and try to copulate with them, ignoring the female herself. The female of the silkworm moth, *Bombyx mori*, carries her scent in pouches on each side of her body. When the liquid from these pouches is squeezed on to paper, the male moth will try to copulate with the paper.

Experiments in varnishing the antennæ of male moths have shown that the males so treated become oblivious to the presence of females close to them, even in species which have a marked "assembling" faculty. A male moth with one of its antennæ removed will fly in circles and spirals and eventually find the female.

It has been found that if one male among a crowd of suitors is allowed access to an imprisoned female, and pairs with her, the other males disperse with one accord. This would seem to indicate that the emanation of the female ceases from the moment of mating. Exceptions to this rule are seen in species which copulate several times.

Among "assembling" species, the Emperor, *Saturnia pavonia* (Plate X and 69, 70), deserves attention. Not only is it one of our largest and handsomest moths, but it is our one native representative of a family hailing from India, Japan and China, of which one member, the Atlas Moth, is the largest moth in the world. The splendour of these oriental creatures, their desert yellow and brown and purple, is, in our Emperor, softened to cloudy colours, as befits one who flies in a misty land. The male is perhaps the handsomer of the two, by reason of its plumed antennæ, rich colouring of chocolate and white, and lower wings suffused with orange. The female is beautifully marked with soft clouds of grey and wavy grey lines on a background of white. All four wings in both sexes bear a central eye-spot, surrounded by concentric circles which, from their fancied resemblance to the ringed planet Saturn, give the moth its family name. These eyes are, perhaps, a protective device, intended to frighten away enemies.

All the caterpillars of the Saturnid moths spin large cocoons (Plate X), composed of a rough outer covering, and a fine inner case. The inner cocoon of some foreign species can be unwound, and the silk thus obtained is used commercially, but its brown strands are of a much coarser texture than the flossy golden and white skeins of the silkworm.

PLATE X.

Top left: CATERPILLAR OF EMPEROR MOTH AMONG BRAMBLE LEAVES MARKED BY LEAF-MINE. *Centre:* MALE EMPEROR MOTH. *Lower centre:* FEMALE EMPEROR MOTH. *Lower right:* COCOON CONSTRUCTED BY THE CATERPILLAR

The cocoon of our Emperor serves no utilitarian purpose save that of protecting its inmate from harm. It is cunningly devised to prevent enemies from getting in, while allowing the moth to get out. Inside the rough outer covering is the thinner case, composed of stiff parallel strands which converge towards the entrance. These separate as the moth crawls out, and close again behind it, leaving the empty pupa case inside, and the cocoon, to all outward appearances, as before.

The inventor of this contraption is a large bright green caterpillar marked with black and adorned with tubercles, from which sprout hairs. It has something of the chameleon's attributes, for the tubercles are pink when it feeds on the heather, green when it feeds on the bramble and meadowsweet.

The Emperor flies by day and can not infrequently be seen zigzagging to and fro on heathery lands in Suffolk, in Ashdown Forest and on the Yorkshire moors. But the Empress flies chiefly at night. She glues her eggs in neat batches to the stems of plants, sometimes to a stone. These moths cannot feed, for they have no tongues. The green-stuff eaten by the caterpillar has to suffice for the sustenance of the moth; when the store is exhausted, the insect dies.

Another "assembling" species is the Oak Eggar, *Lasiocampa quercus* (72, 73), which belongs to the *Lasiocampidae*. Characteristic of this family are its hairy caterpillars, and the difference in size and colouring between the male and female moths of most of its species. The antennæ of the male are plumed, those of the female slender, adorned with a slight fringe.

The male Oak Eggar is chocolate brown in colour, with yellowish bands: the female is larger than the male and her wings are ochreous yellow, with darker transverse bands and a central dot of white.

My chief acquaintance with this moth has been in Suffolk, where the males could be seen dashing to and fro in the sunlight and alighting with such violence that it was a wonder they were not damaged by the impact. They flew chiefly between ten o'clock in the morning and two o'clock in the afternoon; and it was then that they "assembled" in numbers round a box containing newly emerged females.[1] They came to this box, placed inside an open window, a few hours before the first female had left her cocoon. I opened the box and allowed males to enter; they paired immediately with the females. Copulation lasted only twenty minutes to half an hour. Then the pairs separated and the males seemed as anxious to leave their wives as they had been to find them. The females laid their eggs next day.

The name of Oak Eggar does not seem a very apposite one, for the furry caterpillars (73) (which hibernate through the winter) feed on the ivy, bramble, hawthorn and wayfaring tree. The moth's French name of "Banded monk" is more descriptive of its dun-coloured robe.

---

[1] For a thrilling account of the assembling of moths, see *Social Life in the Insect World*, by J. H. Fabre, (Pelican books), chapters "the Great Peacock", and "the Oak Eggar, or Banded Monk".

Both the caterpillar and the moth of the Grass Eggar, *Bombyx trifolii*, are rather similar in appearance to the Oak Eggar. The Small Eggar, *Eriogaster lanestris*, is a much smaller moth, with white-banded, thinly scaled wings of a cocoa-brown. Its caterpillars are gregarious and live during summer in a web cocoon on sloe or hawthorn. You can recognise them by their hairy coats of chocolate and yellow. The slate-blue, orange-striped caterpillars of the allied and rather similar Lackey Moth, *Malacosoma neustria*, are also gregarious, and spin webs which have a messy appearance on fruit-trees in orchards, and on the sloe and sallow of hedgerows in May and June. The female Lackey glues her eggs (75) in a neat "bracelet" round a twig, where they may withstand the rigours of winter and hatch in April.

A few years ago, the Wiltshire Downs were peopled, for several successive summers, by a number of the large and furry caterpillars of the Fox Moth, *Macrothylacia rubi*. Now, there is not one to be seen. The ichneumon fly (18, 19, 78), is probably responsible for their disappearance. I am consoled by the thought that the caterpillar is still common near by in lanes and rough grassy places, and also on moors in Scotland, where it feeds on the rock rose.

The eggs of the Fox moth (59) are laid about June in batches, sometimes in a "bracelet" round a stem, or on a stone. The caterpillars hatch in July; they grow quickly, and when disturbed roll in a ring and fall to the roots of the grass. When small, their hairy bodies are alternately ringed with black and yellow, which changes after a few moults to a body of velvet black covered with a double coat of rippling glossy hairs—some short and tawny, the others brown, much longer, and apt, as I have found, to bring out a nettlerash on the hands that touch them. These caterpillars must be very sensitive, for they invariably die if kept indoors. I found that the only way to rear them was out-of-doors, on a patch of turf transplanted to a flower-pot, and covered in by a gauze awning raised on sticks and tied round the pot. Here my caterpillars thrived—fed with bramble-leaves, and hawthorn, as I could never be quite sure which of the downland plants was their food. About the middle of September they crept down into the grass roots and there lay torpid until the following March, when they emerged to sun themselves, though not to feed, and to spin, among the grass-stems, rough brown cocoons. The moths appeared in May or early June. The round-winged, reddish-grey male, with his handsome plumed antennæ, and the larger, lighter-coloured female, with her antennæ slightly fringed, have all the marks of an "assembling" species, and practise it.

I have found the caterpillars of the Drinker Moth, *Philudoria potatoria*, feeding on coarse grasses, on the banks of ditches and by the riverside in June. Though not gregarious, the caterpillars resulting from the same batch of eggs seldom stray and are usually to be found browsing together in small "herds". They are thirsty creatures, fond of a drop of

72 Oak Eggar, *Lasiocampa quercus*

[*Magnification* × 2

74 Woolly Bear Caterpillar of the Garden Tiger Moth
Arctia caja

73 Oak Eggar, *Lasiocampa quercus*
Caterpillar

rain or dew. You can recognise them by their fur coats, which grow in
dark tufts, with white tufts along the sides and a plume near the tail;
there are, also, broken yellowish stripes along the back. The caterpillar
becomes full-fed in June and spins a long, tapering cocoon attached to a
grass stem. The moth emerges in July and the eggs are laid soon afterwards on a stem or leaf of grass. Here the young caterpillars browse until

Mating Oak Eggar Moths. *Lasiocampa quercus*
(Less than life-size)

the autumn, when they hibernate, to reappear and feed again in April.
The Drinker Moth, with its furry body and ochreous yellow colouring, is
not unlike the oak-eggar, but is slightly smaller and less heavy in build.
Its upper wings are pointed and bear two white marks and a dark diagonal
line. Both sexes fly by night.

These fine big moths, the Drinkers, Foxes and Eggars, have a still larger
and handsomer ally—the Lappet, *Gastropacha quercifolia* (77). This is, in
all its stages, a most curious and striking creature. It begins life as an
oval-shaped, white egg, ringed with green and brown like a bull's-eye

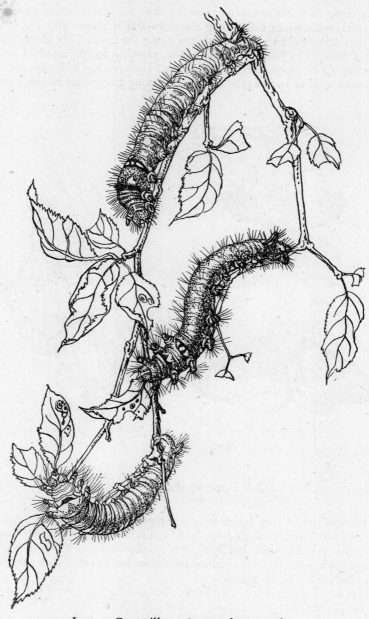

Lappet Caterpillars, *Gastropacha quercifolia*
(*Life-size*)

76 Young Caterpillars of the Brown-tail Moth
Euproctis chrysorrhaea

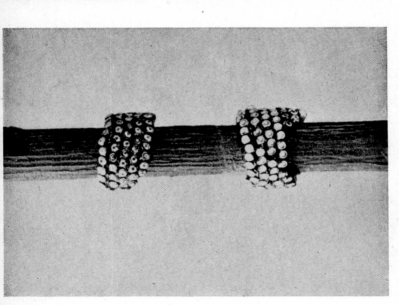

75 Eggs of the Lackey Moth, *Malacosoma neustria*

[*Larger than life*

77 Lappet Moth, *Gastropacha quercifolia*

[*Magnification* × 2]

sweet (79). From this object, which is laid on the underside of a leaf of the red-leaved prunus or the plum, emerges, in July, a dark-grey caterpillar with a thick coat of short hairs. It feeds at night and rests during the day flattened along a twig, which it clasps so tightly that it appears more like a thickening of the wood than a living caterpillar. It grows slowly, and by the end of September is not more than an inch and a quarter long. Although leaves are still plentiful, it now becomes torpid, and, still clinging to its twig, sleeps on through the winter, buffeted by winds, congealed with snow, but never relaxing its hold, until April awakes it to a warm world full of fresh young leaves.

As I write this, a pale March sun is beginning to revive both caterpillars and men from the rigours of the coldest winter for a hundred and fifty years. In February, after a temperature of four and five degrees below zero, rain froze as it fell and covered the land with a sheet of ice. Trees became fantastic, gleaming ice-shapes, wonderful to behold. Each bramble-leaf, each frond of fern, was encased in crystal. Shining, brittle fringes depended from grasses, and the knapweed heads were needled with silver. But this beauty was cruel to living and growing things. Branches were torn off the trees by the weight of the ice. Rabbits and hares froze as they slept, and were picked up encased in ice, and small birds were frozen to branches. I wrote for news of my Lappet caterpillars, wintering on a prunus-tree in the country. They were imbedded in ice, like flies in amber. A week later, heavy snow rendered the countryside impassable and the trees were bowed under its load. But the Lappets are still there, gripping their twigs. No doubt they will begin to feed as soon as the leaves sprout. and I shall watch them grow to a length of four inches, and puzzle over the probable use of the fleshy protuberances, or "lappets" that they bear on their sides, under a fringe of hair. In June they will spin, among the branches, their tight-fitting cocoons of silk and hairs, and in July I shall see the moth, which is like no other.[1] When resting, it gathers its ample wings round its body with the scalloped lower pair drooping in a bird-like attitude, which gives it the German name of "the Brooding Hen".

Who does not know the Garden Tiger, *Arctia caja* (Plate VIII)? It is a splendid creature, with its creamy upper wings patterned with dark brown and its scarlet lower wings spotted with inky black. Its "woolly bear" caterpillars (74) were the first pets of my childhood. Unperturbed by the cramped quarters of a jam-pot tied down with gauze, they thrived on a diet of dead-nettle and never failed to delight me by rolling up like hedgehogs and "shamming dead" when disturbed. In their wild state, these "Bears" feed also on dock, dandelion, hawthorn and on hollyhock. They are very sensitive to vibrations and immediately drop off their food-plant if they feel a rustling in the undergrowth on the approach of heavy feet. You may find them, after hibernation, in spring, sunning themselves

---

[1] My Lappets survived and pupated and the moths emerged in due course.

Male and Female Cream-spot Tiger Moths
Arctia villica
with caterpillar, cocoon and chrysalis
(*Less than life-size*)

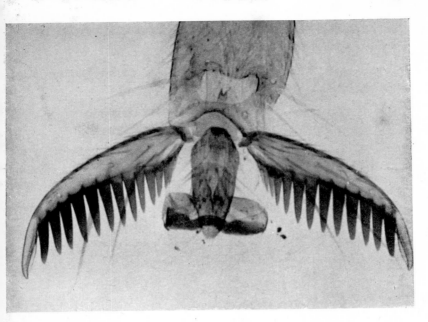

78 Foot of an Ichneumon Fly: showing how well adapted it is for seizing prey

[Highly magnified

79 Eggs of the Lappet Moth, *Gastropacha quercifolia*

COLOUR: GREEN AND BROWN   *[Highly magnified*

80 Caterpillar of the December Moth, *Poecilocampa populi*

This moth, of the family *Lasiocampidae*, is on the wing in October, November, and December, in woods, and is sometimes to be found round gas-lamps. The eggs are laid in winter on the bark of trees, whitethorn, poplar, lime, and oak; on the leaves of which the caterpillar feeds in May and June. This species is widely distributed, but not common

[*Magnification* × 1½]

on a bank or on a fence or wall near their food plant. They pupate inside cocoons of silk and hair.

English country people used to regard these caterpillars as creatures of evil. If you should be so unfortunate as to get one coiled round your finger — said they — you will never be able to get it off again and you will gradually waste away. The same superstition obtained in France, where the caterpillars were (and still may be) known as "Anneaux du Diable".

The fascination of the Garden Tiger is enhanced by its variation. No two specimens are exactly alike. Sometimes the upper wings are creamy, with a few dark marks, and the black shows only as specks on the scarlet lower wings. Sometimes the dark brown obscures the cream, and the black spreads like ink-spills over the scarlet. These extreme aberrations are, of course, rare.

There are several other Tiger Moths, all belonging to the family *Arctiidae*. The handsome cream-spot Tiger, *Arctia villica* (Plate VIII), has yellow underwings spotted with black and a red and yellow body. Its "woolly

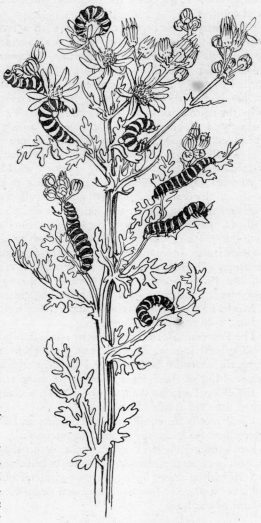

Cinnabar, *Callimorpha jacobaeae*,
Caterpillars on Ragwort
(*Life-size*)

bear" caterpillars feed on groundsel, chickweed and other weeds and can be recognised by their red heads and legs. The Scarlet Tiger, *Panaxia dominula*, is a beauty with dark green iridescent upper wings spotted with cream and scarlet lower wings blotched with black. The furry caterpillar has a yellow stripe down the back and sides, and feeds on the dead-nettle and comfrey.

The hairy, dark brown caterpillar with a reddish line down its back, that you so often see hurrying along roads, or across garden paths in early autumn, is that of the White Ermine, *Spilosoma lubricipeda*. It is on the look-out for a suitable spot, where it spins a thin cocoon effectively concealed by an outer covering of earth. The cream-coloured, black-dotted, yellow-bodied moth emerges in June and is common everywhere. Its ally, the equally common Buff Ermine, *Spilosoma lutea*, has a deeper ground-colour and its black dots are arranged in a diagonal line instead of being sprinkled at random, as in the other. You can recognise another relation, the Muslin Moth, *Cycnia mendica*, by its smaller size, white body and diaphanous white wings sparsely speckled with black.

Another familiar member of this family is the Cinnabar, *Callimorpha jacobaeae*. Its orange and black-ringed caterpillars are often seen on flowering ragwort, in waste places, and sometimes on groundsel in gardens. When full-fed, they construct slight cocoons just below the surface of the ground, and the red and black moth, which flies by day, emerges in June. It appeared once in numbers on the north-east coast, suggesting a sudden invasion. The idea that it sometimes migrates is supported by the capture, off the Norfolk coast, at lightships well away from land, of several specimens, which may have been travelling either to or from the land.

Moths of the *Arctiidae* family cannot feed, for they have no tongues, or, at best, only rudimentary ones.

The Footman Moths (which form a sub-family of the *Arctiidae*) are odd-looking little insects. When at rest, with their long, narrow wings folded along their slender bodies, they look very stiff and straight; hence their name. Most of them are drab-coloured; some are speckled. The prettiest is the Rosy Footman, *Miltochrista miniata*, a charming little moth, coral-tinted, like the inside of a shell.

These moths are equipped with tongues and fly by night. Their hairy caterpillars feed, usually from August onwards through the winter, on lichens growing on trees, or on rocks, or on the ground, and spin silken cocoons in crevices of bark or other nooks and crannies. If kept in captivity they should be reared in a glass-topped metal box, containing their food, and, also, a piece of frequently changed damp blotting-paper placed on the bottom of the box.

CHAPTER XVI

The Geometers (Geometridae)

LET us look at those oddities, the "loopers" and the "stick" caterpillars, and at their elegant, wide-winged moths. These form a large and varied family; the *Geometridae*, in common parlance, the Geometers.

The "loopers", "span-worms", or "measuring-worms" are so called from their gait. Most caterpillars have five pairs of "clasper" legs and walk

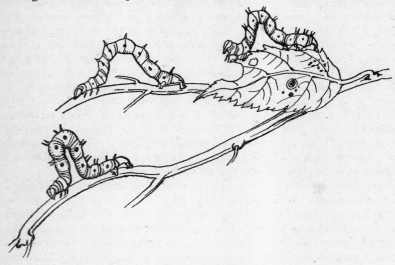

Looper Caterpillars
(*Life-size*)

with an undulating movement; but the "looper" possesses two pairs only, at the end of its body, with a long gap between them and its six "true" front legs, and it has a different way of getting about. First it stretches its body forward, first to one side, then to the other, as though measuring the distance. It then grasps with its front legs and draws up its hind claspers close to them, arching its body into a loop. This measuring and arching proceed alternately and the caterpillar progresses at a considerable pace by these curious strides.

There are a large assortment of loopers. Some feed on the foliage of trees—the hawthorn, sloe, beech, hazel or sallow. Others are to be found on low-growing plants, such as the trefoil, chickweed and bedstraw. They remain on their food-plants during the day, but feed at night. Some of them draw the leaves of trees together with silken threads to form a shelter. Many hibernate through the winter; others feed during the summer and spend the winter in the pupal state, among moss, or underground, in an earthen cocoon.

The resulting moths form several groups. There is a group of "Waves" another of "Pugs" another of "Carpets" and a small, select group of "Emeralds" and many others, numberless as the leaves of the trees among which they hide. All are slender-bodied moths. The females of several are wingless, but most species have wide, butterfly-like wings and rest during the day, head upwards, flattened against walls or fences or foliage, with their wings half expanded in the form of a triangle.

I have always been charmed by the Pugs. They are so tiny, and so exquisite, with their pencilled wings that are occasionally fringed. The Lime-speck Pug, *Eupithecia centaureata*, is like a puff of grey smoke. The Netted Pug, *Eupithecia venosata*, has a pattern as of tiny rivers meandering over its wings. The caterpillars of some of these little creatures feed on flowers. The Lime-speck chooses the petals of the ragwort, scabious and knapweed. The Foxglove Pug, *Eupithecia pulchellata*, lives in the flowers of the foxglove, and feeds therein on the stamens and immature seeds. It enters by boring through the side wall, and then fastens the lower lobe of the flower to the upper one with silken threads. What pleasanter habitation can be imagined? The prettiest of all the Pugs is, I think, the Green Pug, *Chloroclystis rectangulata*, which is bright green, threaded with wavy lines of brown. The caterpillar feeds on apple blossom in May, and pupates in an earthen cocoon, and the moth appears in July.

Unrelated to the Pugs—for it belongs to another Geometer sub-family— is an uncommon viridian green moth, large and most lovely: *Hipparchus papilionaria*, the Large Emerald (81). Its vivid colouring is sadly transitory and fades to a dingy yellow a few months after the moth is dead. The caterpillar rests throughout the winter on a carpet of silk woven near the tip of a twig of the beech, birch or hazel. It is disguised by a colouring of leaf-green tinted with reddish-brown on the head and hind-parts that are in touch with the twig. June is spent in the pupal state, in a cocoon woven among leaves.

Three smaller, less conspicuous moths belonging to this group are the blue-green Grass Emerald, *Pseudoterpna pruinata*, the greenish-white Little Emerald, *Iodis lactearia*, and the olive-green Common Emerald, *Hemithea æstivaria*.

I have an affection for the "Carpets". They appear first in May and remind me of the glory of late spring, with bluebells and campion in drifts of blue and red and woodlands full of song. Among the bluebells grow dog's mercury and hazel saplings, on the leaves of which the carpet moths rest, ingeniously disguised as bird-droppings. A splash of distinct black and white takes shape as the Argent and Sable, *Eulype hastata*. (You may find its caterpillar in rolled-up leaves of birch, and its pupa among moss at the foot of the tree.) A smaller smudge reveals the mottled, grey and

81 Large Emerald, *Hipparchus papilionaria*

[*Magnification* × 1½]

83 Treble-bar Moth, *Anaitis plagiata*

82 Broken-barred Carpet Moth, *Electrophaes corylata*, resting on lichen

white wings of the Common Carpet, *Epirrhoe alternata*, the caterpillar of which feeds on the bedstraw. The Beautiful Carpet, *Mesoleuca albicillata*, is an exceedingly pretty moth with its wings of mealy white, and their dark tips and dark basal patches. It appears in June, after eight months as a pupa, under ground in an earthen cocoon, and it lays its eggs on the bramble and the raspberry.

Differently patterned, but with the family likeness, are the Galium Carpet, *Epirrhoe galiata*, and the pretty Chalk Carpet, *Melanthia procellata*, the caterpillar of which feeds on the Traveller's Joy.

There are a variety of other Carpets, green and grey, brown and reddish and straw-coloured. The Green Carpet, *Colostygia pectinataria*, mottled with a lichen-like pattern of green, grey and black, is one of the prettiest. The allied Yellow Shell, *Euphyia bilineata*, is very common in hedgerows and thickets in July. Its caterpillar feeds on sorrel, hibernates throughout the winter and pupates in May in an earthen cocoon.

July brings also the Dark Umber, *Philereme transversata*—which hides among buckthorn bushes, where the caterpillar feeds between fastened leaves—and the July High-flier, *Hydriomene furcata*, which flattens its olive-and-umber wings against the leaves of the elm. Its eggs, laid in August on the alder and sallow, hatch in May and the caterpillar pupates in earth. The straw-coloured Spinach, *Lygris mellinata*, rests among currant bushes. The caterpillar may be found on the underside of the leaves.

Left: Silver-ground Carpet, *Xanthorhoë montanata*
Top: Clouded Border, *Lomaspilis marginata*
Bottom: Beautiful Carpet, *Mesoleuca albicillata*
(*Life-size*)

There are several Geometer moths that appear, misguidedly, in bleak winter. Not for them the leafy shelter of summer trees; the Early Moth, *Theria rupricaria*, has to be content with the bare hedgerows, the icy nights of January, and the Pale Brindled Beauty, *Phigalia pedaria*, may be found on tree-trunks at this inclement time of year. The Mottled Umber, *Erannis defoliaria*, and the Winter Moth, *Operophtera brumata*, appear from November to February. The wings of the males are faintly coloured with winter browns and greys; but the Spring Usher, *Erannis leucophaearia*, comes with the turn of the year, and shows, in its opalescent wings, a hope of spring. The females of these moths are either wingless, or so inadequately winged as to be unable to fly, and rest on palings or on tree-trunks, often creeping into crevices of bark and bough. They lay their eggs on the bark of the tree, and the newly hatched caterpillars have to crawl some distance to find their food.

"Stick" Caterpillars of Peppered Moth
Biston betularia
(Life-size)

Nature is a fantasy, where the beautiful and grotesque grow side by side. Nowhere are contrasts more evident than among the freakish "stick" caterpillars, and their lovely moths. Their pupae, which are usually found underground, are as squat and compact as the caterpillars are long and thin.

The disguise of the caterpillars is perfect. The green or brownish skin, scored and wrinkled like the bark of the tree; the knots and swellings that simulate buds, and the long, jointed body, all are fashioned in exact imitation of a twig. Clinging by their two pairs of hind claspers, these extraordinary creatures rest stiffly extended, rigid and motionless as the branch that supports them. And how strong they are! Short of hurting them, you cannot dislodge their grip. Scientists tell us that, when clinging to a twig, the pull of a caterpillar is equal to ninety-two times its own weight. The strongest are said to be those living on roses.

85 Wingless Female of the Dotted Border Moth,
Erannis marginaria, hiding in a crevice of bark

[*Magnification* × 2]

84 The Caterpillar of the Orange Moth, *Angerona
prunaria*. A perfect "stick"

[*Very slightly larger than life*]

86 Lilac Beauty Moth, *Hygrochroa syringaria*, showing its curiously twisted wings

[*Magnification* × 2½]

One of these knobbed "sticks" feeds on hawthorn and plum in late summer, and again after hibernation in May, and becomes the Orange

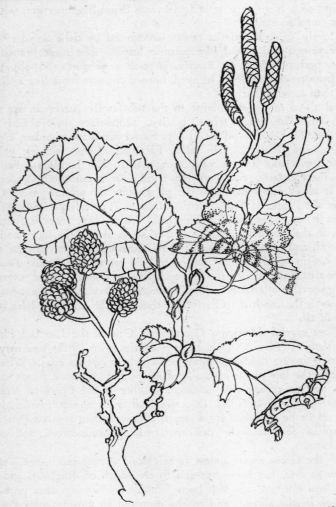

Early Thorn Moth, *Selene bilunaria*, and its stick-like Caterpillar
on an Alder spray
(*Life-size*)

Moth, *Angerona prunaria* (84). Another results in the swift-flying Swallow-tail Moth, *Ourapteryx sambucaria* (Plate IX)—an ethereal creature with wide, curved, butterfly-wings coloured like the lime blossom round which it swoops on sultry July nights. A smaller "twig" becomes that bright yellow, common, but pretty moth, the Brimstone, *Opisthograptis luteolata*. This insect bears on its abdomen, near the wings, a curious organ, consisting of a membrane stretched over a drum-like aperture, which is thought to be an ear.

The lovely "Thorn" moths can be recognised by their angular wings, that are veined and tinted like autumn leaves. The most beautiful of them is, perhaps, the Lilac Beauty, *Hygrochroa syringaria* (86–90), which results from an extraordinary lumped, horned creature more like a Chinese dragon than a caterpillar.

Several allied moths, belonging to the sub-family *Boarminae*, are to be found in London, where elms, birches, plum-trees, privet and lilacs provide food for the caterpillars. I have found the Waved Umber, *Hemerophila abruptaria* (Plate IX), in May, flattened against wooden palings, where it looks like a strip of peeling bark. The handsome Brindled Beauty, *Lycia hirtaria*, rests on elm-trunks in Kensington Gardens in April. It sometimes remains in the pupal state for several years. Commoner is the Peppered Moth, *Biston betularia*. Typical specimens of this moth are white, "peppered" with black; but a black form is found in London, in the industrial districts of Yorkshire, and in the south and east of England, and in Scotland, and is now much commoner than the type. This melanism was formerly thought to be a protective disguise assumed by moths that dwelt among the soot and grime of cities. Recent investigations suggest that the black coloration becomes increasingly frequent the farther north the moth is to be found; those of the Shetland Isles being blackest of all.

There are several day-flying Geometers. One is the Latticed Heath, *Chiasma clathrata* (Plate IX). It belongs to the open lands; you may see it fluttering among fields of clover, on which it lays its eggs. When at rest, among the low plants of chalky slopes, its criss-crossed wings vanish into the pattern of the dry grasses. Another is the Speckled Yellow, *Pseudopanthera macularia* (Plate IX), which flies in sunny woodlands in June; it might be mistaken for a small, yellow, brown spotted butterfly. Its caterpillar feeds on the dead-nettle, hedge-woundwort, and other labiate plants.

Few of the Geometridae appear to migrate. A rare moth, the Vestal, *Rhodometra sacraria*, has been captured in the south of England, and the Gem, *Cidaria obstipata*, has also been found. The immigration probably takes place in the spring, and moths captured in autumn may be the descendants of spring migrants.

88 The Lilac Beauty, *Hygrochroa syringaria*, always has the old skin of the caterpillar attached to the pupa case. The pupa itself is enclosed in a very fine network of silk   [*Life-size*

87 The Lilac Beauty's (*Hygrochroa syringaria*) Caterpillar makes a silken bag as support for the pupa

[*Rather larger than life*

90 Caterpillar of the Lilac Beauty, *Hygrochroa syringaria*, never still, but sways backwards and forwards, continued.

89 A Lilac Beauty, *Hygrochroa syringaria*, Caterpillar

CHAPTER XVII

Primitive Moths and Tree-boring Caterpillars (Cossidae, Sesiidae and Hepialidae)

BUTTERFLIES and moths appear to us as the familiar spirits of the flowers; and with reason, for their existence depends upon that of the plants, which provide nectar for them and food for their caterpillars. This alliance was formed aeons ago. The butterflies and moths and the plants are contemporaries and have developed side by side; their origins can be traced to the Mesozoic period.

You will remember that this was an epoch more recent than the Carboniferous age: the butterflies and moths are therefore a younger race than the grasshoppers and dragon-flies, which date from the time when coal was a growing forest. We do not know what the first butterfly looked like, for butterflies make poor fossils; but it is certain that moths and butterflies as we now know them are as distinct from the aboriginal type as our present-day plants are different from the giant ferns and the enormous club-mosses and horsetails of the coal forests. Here and there, however, primitive forms still survive. Among plants they are to be seen in the Equisetums, or horse-tails, that grow in swampy meadows, and among moths in the Swifts or *Hepialidae*. These insects are thought to have originated in the Caddis-flies, a division of the order *Neuroptera*. The shape and proportion of their long, narrow wings is more that of a dragon-fly than of a moth, and their antennæ are short and inconspicuous. Their maggot-like caterpillars feed on the roots of grasses and of various plants—the hop, burdock, dandelion and dead-nettle. The largest of the Swifts is the ghost moth, *Hepialus humuli*. You may see these curious insects at dusk, silently swaying over the grasses; ghosts they seem indeed, that have strayed into the present from the mists of the earth's beginning. The whitish males dance up and down; the females fly straight and have orcheous upper wings and lower wings of nebulous grey.

There is also an Orange Swift, *Hepialus sylvina*, a smaller insect of the woodlands, where it flies at dusk over bracken, on the roots of which the caterpillar feeds. The commonest member of the group is *Hepialus lupulina*, the Common Swift. As I have told you, its caterpillar sometimes makes serious depredations.

The Gold Swift, *Hepialis hectus*, shows, in the male, an extraordinary scent-organ on the hind leg, which is clothed in long, dense fringes of hair. When at rest, the leg lies in a groove in the abdomen; but when the male flies, pendulum-wise, to and fro in its love-flight, the hind legs hang down and the scent streams out.

Very curious, with their transparent wings—hardly recognisable, indeed, as moths—are the Clear-wings. The Hornet Moth, *Sesia apiformis*, has a yellow and black striped body which resembles that of its ferocious namesake, from which it differs in having red legs. The maggot-like caterpillar spends two years feeding on the roots and inside the stems of poplars, on the trunk of which the newly emerged moth may be found on sunny mornings in May and June. The Currant Clear-wing, *Aegeria tipuliformis*, resembles a small fly. It lays its eggs on the bark of currant-trees, into which the caterpillars burrow and feed on the inner pith, working their way downwards, so that the increasing girth of the stem can accommodate their growth. When full-fed, they gnaw their way to the side of the stem, leaving a thin film of bark, through which the pupa pushes its way when ready to emerge; and the moth creeps out, leaving its empty shell protruding from the hole.

The most extraordinary of the tree-boring caterpillars are those of the Goat Moth, *Cossus cossus* (95). They hatch from eggs laid on the bark and the young caterpillars bore into the wood and make a labyrinth of tunnels inside the tree. They are extremely powerful for their size and are armed with jaws that reduce the wood to powder. It is noticeable that they are never found in a young tree, preferring one that is going back in condition. If you listen near a tenanted willow, or poplar, you will hear a gnawing, like that of mice, proceeding from within, while sawdust drips from the mouths of the tunnels, and you will smell the curious odour, like that of a billy-goat, that gives the moth its name. The old writers called the caterpillar the "Augur-worm". It is said that the Romans roasted "cossus" caterpillars and ate them as a delicacy.

After three years of a diet of sawdust, the caterpillar feels replete, gnaws its way out of the tree and sets off in search of a suitable place for pupation. You may find it at such times. It is a giant among caterpillars and hideously ugly; salmon pink, bald and shiny, with a large polished black head. If you want to watch it, put it into a roomy tin pierced with air holes and give it some rotten wood as material for its cocoon, and some sawdust as food. (Caterpillars reared from the eggs thrive on a diet of sliced potatoes.) In its wild state the caterpillar sometimes makes an earthen cocoon.

The moth, which emerges in July, is a coarse, rugged-looking creature which in repose looks like a knot in the bark. It has large eyes with ten thousand facets, but lacks tongue or mouth-parts and dies after a very short time.

Everyone is familiar with the red-and-black Six-spot Burnet, *Zygaena filipendulae*, that flies in the sunshine in July and August. Its colonies are to be found all over the chalk downs, and on cliffs and sometimes in marshy meadows, where their conspicuous whitish cocoons are attached to grasses. The caterpillars, which are less easily found, feed on clover and on vetches and hibernate through the winter, becoming full-fed in spring. The Burnet moth often flies in company with two small, sunshine-loving Noctuids; the Burnet Companion, *Ectypa glyphica*, a purple-brown moth with yellow streaks on its lower wings, and the rather similar, but more distinctly marked Mother Shipton, *Euclidemera mi*. The pattern on its upper wings has a resemblance to the hooked nose and nutcracker jaws of a witch; it is also rather like the letter M, hence the moth's English and specific names.

There are various aberrations of the Six-spot Burnet. In one, the crimson spots of the upper wings run together to form a blotch. Other varieties have spots and lower wings of yellow or orange. The Six-spot Burnet is easily confused with two allied and very similar species. the Five-spot Burnet, *Zygaena trifolii*, and the Narrow-bordered Five-spot Burnet, *Zygaena lonicerae*. All these Burnets possess clubbed antennæ, a feature which is found in no other family of moths.

The Burnet Moth is sluggish in the mornings, and does not fly until the sun shines; hence its old name of "the Ten-o'clock Sleeper".

Six-spot Burnet Moth, *Zygaena filipendulae*, with Cocoon on Knapweed
(Life-size)

Flying in the sunshine, on chalk hills in May and June, you may find a pretty little greenish-bronze moth, allied to the Burnets: the Forester, *Procris statices*. Like the Burnets, it lives in colonies. Its toothed antennæ are thickened at the tip.

And now I must leave you, to make your own discoveries in the world of moths. Perhaps you will find beauties that space has not allowed me to describe in this book; the Hook-tips, with their curved wings that are patterned like shells, or the Green Pea and its allies, or the lovely Peach-blossom. Perhaps your attention will be claimed by the great company of the Microlepidoptera. Wherever your enthusiasms may lead, new wonders will unfold; there is ever something new to be learnt about the humblest of moths. You will gaze, and marvel, and give thanks for the miracle of Life.

93 Eggs of Common Marbled
Carpet Moth, *Dysstroma truncata*
LAID

COLOUR: WHITE   [*Magnification* × 35]

94 Eggs of Common Marbled
Carpet Moth *Dysstroma truncata*
HATCHED

COLOUR: DEAD WHITE

[*Magnification* × 35]

92 Eggs of Waved Umber Moth
Hemerophila abruptaria
COLOUR: DEEP PURPLISH, WITH WHITE DOTS AT
ANGLES OF OCTAGONS

[*Magnification* × 30]

91 Eggs of Scarce Tissue Moth
Calocalpe cervinatus
COLOUR: SEMI-TRANSPARENT GREENISH WHITE

[*Magnification* × 20]

95 Goat Moth, *Cossus cossus*, on woodland path, having just emerged.
Chrysalis can be seen sticking up out of the ground

[*Magnification* × 2

PART III

CHAPTER XVIII

Notes on Collecting, Setting and Storing Butterflies and Moths

A WELL-ORDERED collection of butterflies and moths, of your own taking and setting, is an achievement of which you may justly be proud; for it is both decorative and instructive. Though the butterflies have lost the fluid grace of life, yet they keep something of the charm that belongs to all natural objects. To this their precise and formal arrangement adds an artificial elegance. They please after the manner of a piece of embroidery, or a tapestry. Theirs is the rich diversity of a mosaic, or a formal garden. To the pleasure of the eye is added that of association. In contemplating them, you recall the glory of past summers, or the lifting of clouds after days of wind and rain, when the butterflies seemed to have forsaken, for ever, the desolate scene.

In the rows of outspread butterflies you may study at leisure the venation of wings, the shapes of antennæ. You may see the spring and summer forms of some butterflies and the variations apparent in others of the same season but from different neighbourhoods. Richly patterned Marsh Fritillaries from Devon are aligned near the duskier Dorset type. Silver-washed Fritillaries from Essex show a yellower ground-colour when compared with contemporaries from the New Forest and from Cranborne Chase, where the males are almost orange and show much variety in their black markings, particularly in the row of spots, sometimes distinct, sometimes confluent, of the border of their hind wings. Chalkhill Blues from different downlands are variously spotted on their under-surface, some being slashed with black, others asymetrically spotted, or, occasionally, without any spots at all. Green-veined Whites of spring and summer, from Wiltshire, from Suffolk, with Scotch forms and Irish forms, are an assembly variously clad in the elegance of black and white. Here is a group of Meadow Browns, some dark as soot, others so faintly tinted as to be more the colour of wood-ash than of the earth near which they habitually rest.

A couple of summers' diligent collecting in different parts of England will yield an assortment of the common butterflies with their seasonal and local variations. Patience and perseverence are needed where the rare butterflies, the extreme variations, are sought for. But now and then you may come across a freak; a Peacock without eyes,[1] a small Copper with a

---

[1] The appearance of aberrations, and the reasons for their abnormality, opens out a fascinating field for exploration. For we learn, from the researches of scientists, that the colour and pattern of the wings is determined at a certain period of the pupal

creamy ground-colour, or an all-black White Admiral. These extreme aberrations are much sought after by collectors and entomological dealers and fetch prices that range from £1 to £10 (or more) in the auction room when large collections are split up and sold.

But before going out to catch your butterflies, see that all is ready at home for setting and storing them. You will need hinged store-boxes, cork- and paper-lined, or, better still (if you can afford it), a cabinet with glazed drawers. Setting boards you must have, of different sizes, to accommodate anything from a Pug to a Death's Head, from a Skipper to a Swallow-tail. Pins are indispensable; black entomological pins of different sizes with heads so small as to be imperceptible when the butterfly is impaled. Other necessaries are a net, a killing-bottle, a relaxing jar, chip-boxes in "nests" that fit into each other, benzine, methylated spirit, camphor or naphthalene, some long darning needles (or embroidery needles) thin tracing-paper, and ordinary pins. If you can, get a pair of entomological forceps, but this is nowadays not easy.

Net, pins, killing-bottle, chip-boxes, cabinet, store-boxes and setting-boards may be obtained either from Messrs. Watkins & Doncaster, 36, Strand, London, W.C.2, or from L. Hugh Newman, Esq., F.R.E.S., The Butterfly Farm, Bexley, Kent. The killing-bottle is a wide-mouthed glass jar closed with a cork stopper. Its lethal properties are due to a small quantity of cyanide of potassium embedded under plaster of paris at the bottom of the jar. This ensures, in insects, a painless death; they fall into a stupor, and expire after an interval that varies with the different species. Fritillaries, Blues, and the Hawk-moths cling tenaciously to life. If taken too soon from the jar, they have a disconcerting way of reviving on the setting-board where, impaled and probably hungry, they wave despairing legs and unfurl a hopeless proboscis. The cyanide loses its potency by degrees, and if the bottle is left uncorked. A well-charged jar should, with care, last for two seasons. Empty jars are sold by entomological stores. Your local chemist would probably fill one for you, if you sign his "poison book", and give him full directions, which are obtainable from either of the addresses I have given.

A relaxing jar can be contrived at home. Press two inches of clean damp sand into the bottom of a screw-top, wide-mouthed, jam or pickle jar. Cut a cork in slices. Fix each slice by a drawing-pin on to a two-sheet thick circle of blotting-paper cut to the circumference of the jar. Damp the blotting-paper, but *not* the corks, push it gently into the jar so that it rests on the sand, and it is ready to receive stiffened insects. Pin these carefully on to the pieces of cork and screw on the lid. Do not let wings or legs touch the blotting-paper or they will become mouldy. Twelve hours should suffice to relax them. Do not leave them longer than twenty-four

stage, and that the life-forces that then imprint their stamp on the developing tissues can be diverged from their normal course if the pupa be subjected to extremes of heat and cold. The perfect insect retains the stamp of these rigours which are apparent in curious and abnormal markings.

hours in the bottle. Renew the sand each time the jar is used, and keep the jar very clean. Blotting-paper and corks may be used several times if kept dry when not in use.

If you prefer the "real thing" you can buy ready-charged relaxing jars from the entomological stores.

Now for the net. This, nowadays, is a simple affair. Not for you the two-handed clap-net, the net disguised as an umbrella, the Emperor-net supported by a network of rigging on a twenty-foot pole, which equipped your forebears for the chase. Your net will be a bag of fine black net, just under a yard long, depending from a stiff hoop of cane bent into a ring, the two ends of which are inserted into the arms of a Y-shaped piece of metal. A straight stick, or bamboo cane, about two foot six inches long thrust into the socket of the Y forms the handle. This net may be bought from the shop, when you will probably be able to get one with a jointed ring; when withdrawn from the Y and from the hem of net, it folds into a small packet, easily stowed into a corner of your week-end case, with the net wrapped round it.

If your means are limited, I would urge you to lay out money first of all on store-boxes or cabinet, killing-bottle and pins. The net may be made at home, the metal Y-piece dispensed with; for if the cane hoop be soaked until pliable, its two ends, straightened, may be lashed to the handle with wire or strong twine.

Net in hand, now sally forth, with killing-bottle and chip-boxes stowed in your coat pockets, or, if the weather be hot, in a haversack or basket. I usually take with me a pencil and drawing-book, wherein I make quick drawings of butterflies in their various positions of feeding, basking, or repose. The line of life is an elusive one, not to be recaptured, hardly even remembered, when the insect is dead. But a quick drawing may fix the flattened curve, the arc like a bent bow, that stretches from tip to tip of the outspread wings of the Fritillary; or the tilt of the perching Blue.

Each species has, too, its own way of standing and of walking The antennæ are differently held on different occasions. When wandering in search of butterflies, remember to approach likely spots with the sun behind you. You will then come upon them with outspread wings. Butterflies always settle with their backs to the sun, which thus illumines each eye equally and gives them the maximum of vision. You will be able to see better yourself, too. The colour of the butterflies will be bright against the background of earth or leaves; whereas if you walk with the sun in your eyes, grasses and foliage will be broken up into patches of light and darkness, wherein the butterflies, inconspicuous in silhouette, are not perceived until your near approach startles them into the flight of escape.

When walking along a sunlit path, see to it that your shadow does not fall on a resting butterfly, for at the sudden darkness it will be off in a moment.

15

Your net may be used in different ways. You can bring it down like an extinguisher, on butterflies resting on the ground, or on flowers. To catch a flying butterfly you must sweep the air with the gesture of a tennis-player hitting a ball. The net will billow out as the butterfly is swept into it, and a turn of the wrist will then fold the muslin over the hoop, with the butterfly imprisoned in the bag. When hurrying to the chase, remember to keep your eye on the butterfly, not on the net. A butterfly in the net usually shuts its wings and can easily be slipped into the killing bottle.

The ordinary net measures about fourteen inches across the top. For taking butterflies or moths on flowers a smaller net is handy. In appearance like a child's toyshop shrimping-net, but with an eight-inch cane handle, you can make it at home. With this light hand-net, insects may be swept off tall plants such as Michaelmas daisies, fleabane and hemp agrimony. But the problem of catching bramble-feasting butterflies will probably remain to vex entomologists as long as blackberries have thorns. For, as you lower the net, these clutch at the gauze, tearing it, impeding your movements, while the coveted Fritillary or White Admiral escapes.

Bramble-feasting butterflies become much engrossed in their meal, and it is sometimes possible to "box" them into a chip-box or killing-bottle. I once caught a superb Valezina with a wire-gauze soup strainer. You will doubtless be able to think out your own method of approach.

When starting a collection, it is well to think out a plan for its arrangements and limitations for, say, the first two seasons. Take only specimens that are needed, or your boxes may become cluttered up with butterflies which might with advantage have been left alive to reproduce their species. After two seasons, when you have a tolerable array before you, gaps can be filled and varieties added to. Take perfect specimens only, and sparingly of these; for our common butterflies are in many varieties now less common than of yore, owing to the ploughing up of waste land and the felling of forests.

Dead butterflies should not be left indefinitely in the killing-bottle, especially if you are walking, as they will jostle against one another to their mutual detriment. Place each dead specimen in a chip-box just large enough to hold it. If you can buy a small cork-lined store-box, about six inches by four inches, take it with you on your excursions and pin into it any butterflies that are ready. Entomological pins can be stuck between the two surfaces of a pair of cardboard discs, covered with velvet or felt and sewn together into the shape of a large button. This portable pin-cushion may be attached by a loop and safety-pin to the lapel of your coat.

The appearance of your collection will depend ultimately upon the setting of the butterflies, so take pains to perfect yourself in this art. See that each pin is thrust exactly through the centre of the thorax, with enough of the tip protruding under the insect to enable you later to affix thereon a tiny triangle or square of paper bearing details of date and place of capture. See that the setting-boards are clean and that the surface is not roughened by previous pin-holes. At the top of each, in the centre of the flat surface, fix, with drawing-pin, pin, or small tack, a strip of tracing paper, or a length of tape, long enough to reach from top to bottom of the board. Stick the impaled insect into the centre of the groove, then, with a not too sharp needle, held in the right hand, separate the closed wings

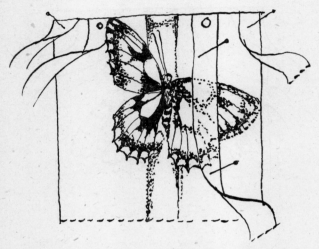

First stage of setting upper surface. The wings
are spread out with a needle and fixed roughly in
position, first one side, then the other
(*Rather larger than life*)

gently and between them insert the paper-strip, or tape, held in the left hand. Tauten this gradually until the wings are flattened on the board. Slip the right-hand needle under the wings, holding it in a horizontal position so as not to tear them, and with it gently push the wings up and down until the right position is obtained. Then pin down the upper strip with ordinary pins. It is well to affix a second strip of paper to hold down the tips of the wings, which sometimes curl up, spoiling the appearance of the butterfly. The antennæ should be spread out in the form of a V and held in place either by pins or another narrow paper strip. The lower margin of the top wings should form a right-angle with the line of the body, and the lower wings should not be dropped too far from the top wings. Their position will depend upon the kind of butterfly set, some having more voluminous hind wings than others.

This "set" position is not the posture adopted by the living butterfly, which often droops its top wings over the lower pair, thus showing the flattened arc that I have mentioned as noticeable in Fritillaries. But the artificial attitude has a neat appearance when the butterflies are arranged in vertical rows, (which must be perfectly straight) with pencil lines ruled between the rows, in the cabinet.

The butterflies should be spaced so that the antennae of each one overlaps slightly the hind wings of the butterfly above. Each species should be represented by male and female, top surface, with male and female,

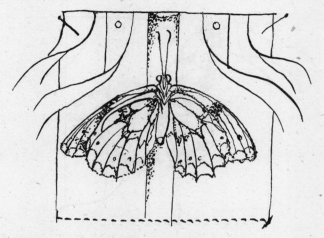

First stage of setting underside. When spread out by means of a not-too-sharp needle, the wings, which were closed over the butterfly's back, rest naturally on the board in this position and can be moved into the correct set position by means of a needle slid under them
(*Rather larger than life*)

underside, of both spring and summer broods and of each local variation that you can discover. To these add any aberrations that are worth keeping. This arrangement applies also to moths, where the series of variations may be numerous.

The wings of moths are as a rule stiffer than most of butterflies and flatten on to the board without much difficulty. But their attachment to the thorax is often so firm as to pull the body out of position when the wings are pinned down. When setting moths, unfold the front pair of legs with the tip of your needle and spread them out in a more or less natural position. I usually unfurl, also, the tongues of some of my specimens, for these show interesting structures, especially among the Hawk-moths.

Large butterflies and moths should be left at least two weeks on the setting-board. Your specimens should be arranged in correct up-to-date scientific order, each with its Latin and English name. The names of families and sub-divisions should head their respective groups. Label lists

for butterflies and moths were at one time to be bought. If now no longer sold owing to paper restrictions, a price list of set butterflies will answer the purpose.

A few balls of naphthalene or a block of camphor should be sewn into a gauze bag and pinned into the corner of each store-box or into the drawers of the cabinet (these are sometimes provided with divisions to hold preservatives). The set butterflies and moths should remain in perfect condition for an indefinite number of years if cabinet and store boxes are kept in a dry room. Never keep them against an outside wall. In wet weather bring them now and then close to the fire and open the boxes and drawers for a few minutes in order to dry and ventilate them. Damp conditions produce mould on wings, legs and antennæ. Once this has appeared it can never be completely eradicated, but it can be checked by an application of methylated spirits, painted on to the mouldy parts with a camel-hair brush.

Thick-bodied moths, such as Puss Moths and some Hawk-moths, exude after a

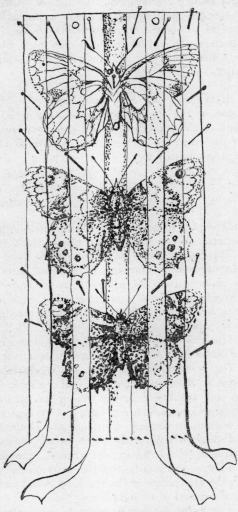

A row of set Butterflies with wings arranged in the correct position

time a fatty substance which spreads on to their wings in greasy patches and drops on to the paper of the drawer. Pure benzine applied lavishly and allowed to soak into blotting-paper placed under the insect will remove stains but leaves the wings with a bedraggled look. The abdomens of Death's Head moths should be snipped off, ripped up along the underside with a pair of sharp embroidery scissors, the contents removed with needles and a sharp crochet-hook, the hollow stuffed with cotton wool and the abdomen glued on again. This is not as difficult as it sounds, and if carefully done the operation leaves no scar. When on the setting-boards specimens should be kept in a drawer, or, better still, in a closed cupboard or chest where they will be safe from the attacks of spiders, earwigs and mice.

I keep a written diary, daily notes of my captures and discoveries, with notes on the annual appearance of each resident species. I note also the date of the appearance of each migrant species, with particulars of time of day, direction of wind, and weather conditions. These particulars are sent in annually to:

Capt. Dannreuther,
Windycroft,
Hastings,

on the printed forms provided by the South-eastern Union of Scientific Societies (Insect Immigration Committee).

This society forms its records partly from the notes of amateur as well as professional entomologists, from all parts of Britain. Particulars may be obtained from the address I have given.

My diary contains a dated record of each stage in the life of the larvæ, some bred from the egg, that I rear in breeding cages or sleeved on plants in the open.

This note-book supplements my collection, and the two together form the sum of my observations from season to season.

The breeding of butterflies and moths from caterpillars and from the egg is an absorbing occupation and one which will provide good specimens for your collection, besides giving you an insight into their life-history. To be successful, it is necessary to keep eggs and larvæ as much as possible in natural conditions. Sunshine and shade, dryness and humidity, heat and cold all have their effect, which varies with each species. Small Tortoiseshell caterpillars like sunshine, provided it is not too strong, and will thrive on a bunch of nettles stuck into a bottle inside a sunny window. But the caterpillars of the Speckled Wood and of the Green-veined White die if exposed to sunlight through glass. In natural conditions they would feed on rather damp grass and cruciferous plants growing in the shade, and it is in shady corners that the female lays her eggs. If taken indoors, eggs and caterpillars must be kept in a cool room in a not too bright light. Their food must be renewed twice a day or it will shrivel. If allowed to become dry the caterpillars do not thrive and eventually die. Caterpillars must not be overcrowded and their abodes should be kept clean, the droppings removed daily with a spoon or brush. A glass-fronted, zinc-sided breeding cage, wooden at top and bottom, with a wooden door, is a useful possession; but it is not a necessity. Most caterpillars thrive in large jam-jars covered with gauze held down by an elastic band. Very young caterpillars should be kept in a small glass-topped box where there is food near at hand so that they can feed without exhausting themselves by wandering about. Caterpillars due to pupate should be given earth in which to burrow, or rubble, or leaves in which to spin a cocoon. Voracious caterpillars and those that are gregarious, thrive best when "sleeved" inside a large muslin bag tied round a bough of their food-plant, which is often a tree or shrub. When the branch is stripped, it can be cut off with the caterpillars on it, and tied on to a fresh leafy bough.

Hibernating butterflies are best kept out-of-doors through the winter, but they must not be allowed to become wet; for these reasons. When hibernating, a caterpillar is fatter than when in an active state. Its body loses some of its water content, and it is upon this desiccation that its powers of resistance partly depend. Other physiological changes contribute to its survival. The colloids in its tissues and body-fluids bind water as films round themselves, and this "bound" water does not freeze until the temperature falls *below* normal freezing-point. The caterpillar is further protected from cold by a system of super-cooling, whereby the remaining water in its body is kept ice-free except in abnormally cold conditions. So keep your hibernating larvæ dry and healthy, in an open but roofed shed, or under the shelter of wide eaves.

I have kept hibernating Cream-spot Tiger caterpillars successfully through a hard winter by housing them in a bottomless bucket placed on the ground, with a double thickness of muslin tied over it to prevent the inroads of earwigs and other predatory creatures. A slate propped over the bucket kept off rain and snow, and screws of paper inside it were at once appropriated by the caterpillars, which emerged from them to pupate in spring.

It is a wise precaution to unearth burrowed pupæ from soil or sand which may become too damp or too dry for their survival and meta-morphosis. They can be kept throughout the winter in cotton-wool in a closed tin, or in a cupboard. Early in March you may slip each pupa head upwards into a twist of paper shaped like a miniature grocer's bag. The bags may be pinned on to a strip of card fixed against the side of a box topped with gauze and furnished with a few branching twigs. Place a piece of wet sponge on the lid of a tin or in a saucer on the bottom of the box, to keep the air humid. The emerging moths (or butterflies, for chrysalises may also be included) find a foothold on the paper and crawl up the sides of the box to dry their wings.

The chrysalises of green-veined Whites need more humidity than those of Large and Small Whites. If allowed to become dry, the butterflies fail to burst their bonds, or emerge as cripples.

The foregoing brief notes record some of my own experiences, and lay down no hard and fast rule for collecting, which is a large subject affording endless opportunities for experiment and research. Look upon your collection as a key to knowledge, a means to an end. For your aim is not accumulation merely, but the study of Life.

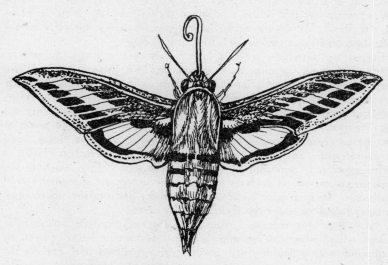

Striped Hawk-moth, *Celerio linea livornica*
(*Slightly larger than life*)

INDEX

The numerals in Roman refer to the colour plates; those in italics refer to the figure numbers of the photographic illustrations.

A B C of Entomology, 1
Abdomen, 3, 103
Aberrations, 107
Abnormality, 107
Accessories (for collecting) 108 et seq.
Acheron, 67
Acherontia atropos, 49, 50, 67
Acronyctinae, 80
Adonis Blue, 27, 26, IV
Aegaria tipuliformis, 104
Africa, Islands off, 15
Aglais urticae, 5–9 1, I
Agrotidae, 80–83
Agrotis ipsilon, 83
Agrotis saucia, 83
Agrotis segetum, 80
"Alderman" Butterfly, 54
Amathes c-nigrum, 80
Amathes diptrapezium, 80
Amathes triangulum, 80
America, 15
American Wainscot, 83
Amyl-acetate, 78
Anaitis plagiata, 83, IX
Anaplectoides prasina, 79
Anatomy of caterpillar, 2
Anatomy of butterflies, 49, 50
Androconia, 4, 34
Angerona prunaria, 101, 84
Angle shades, 79, 65, IX
"Anneaux de Diable", 95
Annulet Moth, 59
Antennæ, 69, 87
Antler Moth, 59
Apamea monoglypha, 79, 61
Apamea lithoxylea, 79
Apatele aceris, 80
Apatele euphorbiae var. myricae, 66, VI
Apatele megacepla 81, 64
Apatele psi, 81
Apatele tridens, 81
Apatura iris, 37, 39, 31
Aphantopus hyperantus, 31, 30, V
Aporia crataegi, 12, 13, 14
April Butterfly, 19
Arctia caja, 93, 74, VIII
Arctia villica, 94, 95, VIII
Arctiinae, 87
Argent and Sable Moth, 98

Argynnids, 52
Argynnis aglaia, 36, VI
Argynnis cydippe, 38
Argynnis euphrosyne, 19, III
Argynnis paphia, 37, 38, 33, VI
Argynnis selene, 19, 7, VI
Aricia agestis, 26, IV
"Assembling", 87 et seq.
Atalanta, 54
Atlas Moth, 88
Attraction to light, 60, 61
Augur Worm, 104
Autumn, 53
Azure Blue Butterfly, 21

"Backgammon-board", 32
"Banded Monk" Moth, 89
Barometric pressure, 43
Bath White, 12
Beautiful Carpet, 99
Bedstraw Hawk-moth, 68
Bee Hawk-moths, 67
"Bee Tiger" Moth, 67
"Beet Army Worm", 83
Biston betularia, 100, 102
Black Arches, 60, 79
Black Hairstreak, 39
Black-veined Brown, 15, 17
Black-veined White, 12, 13, 14
Blue-speckt, 21
Blues, 25 et seq., IV
Bombyx mori, 88
Bombyx trifolii, 90
Breeding caterpillars, 115
Brimstone Butterfly, 9 et seq., 2, 3, 4, 5,
Brimstone Moth, 59
Brindled Beauty, 102
Brindled Green, 82
Broad-bordered Bee Hawk 67
Broad-bordered Yellow Underwing, 81
Broken-barred Carpet Moth, 82, VI
"Brooding Hen". 93
Brown Argus Blue, 26, IV
Brown Hairstreak, 39, 24
Brown-tail, 75, 76
Buff-tip, 70, 73, 57
Burnet Companion, 103
Burnished Brass, 78, VIII

Cabbage Whites, 13, 43, 12, 16
Caddis flies, 103
Caeca, 31
Callimorpha jacobaeae, 95
Callophrys rubi, 23, 23
Calocalpa cervinatus, 91, VI
Camberwell Beauty, 15, 39, 58
Carpets, 60, 98
Carterocephalus palaemon, 35
Catocala nupta, 82, VIII
Celastrina argiolus, 21, IV
Celerio euphorbiae, 68
Celerio galii, 68
Celerio linea livornica, 68, 116
Cerapteryx graminio, 59, 80
Cerura furcula, 71
Cerura hermalina, 71
Cerura vinula, 70, 71, 51, 52
Chalk-hill Blue, 27, 49, 107 IV
"Chenilles cochonnes", 66
Chequered Skipper, 35
Chequered White, 12
Chiasma clathrata, 102, IX
Chlorocystis rectangulata, 98
Chrysalis, 1, 10, 16, 17, 21, 23, 28, 32, 34, 37, 53, 2, 3, 4, 11, 37, 49, 95, I, II, III
Cidaria obstigata, 102
Cinnabar, 95, 96
Claspers, 97
Clays, 80
Clearwings, 104
Clothes Moth, 59
Clouded Yellow, 12, 15
Cocoon, 62, 96, 98, 49, X
Coenonympha pamphilus, 31
Coenonympha tullia, 31
Colias croceus, 12, 15
Collecting butterflies, 107 et seq.
Colostygia pectinataria, 99
Colour vision of butter- flies, 16
Comma Butterfly, 9, 15, 39, 56, 57, 40
Common Blue, 25, 26, 27, 48, 25, IV
Common Marbled Carpet, eggs of, 93, 94
Common Swift, 59, 60, 103
Common Wainscot, 83

Convolvulus Hawk, 68
Cossus cossus, 104, *95*
Courtship of butterflies, 43
Coxcomb Prominent, 73
Cream-spot Tiger, 94, VIII
Cross-pairing, 51
Cucullia umbratica, 84
Cucullia verbasci, 84
Cupido minimus, 26, IV
Currant Clear-wing, 104
Cyanide of potassium, 108
Cycnia mendica, 96

Dagger Moths, 81, VIII
Danaids, 15, 30
Danaus plexippus, 15, *17*
Dark Arches, 78, 79, *61*
Dark Dagger, 81
Dark Sword-grass, 83
Dark Tussock, 74, *56*
Dark Umber, 99
Darts, 79, 80
Darwin, Charles, 14
Dasychira fascelina, 74, *56*
Dasychira pudibunda, 74, 75
Death's Head Hawk-moth,
  59, *49*, *50*
December Moth, *80*
Deilephila elpenor, 66, VII
Deilephila porcellus, 66, *42*
Delicate Moth, 83
Dimorphism, 15
Dingy Skipper, 35
Diptera, 62
Dog's Tooth, 59
Dotted Border, *85*
Double Dart, 80, 81
Double Square-spot, 80
Doubtful Rustic, 59
Drumming, 8, 16, 23, 56
Duke of Burgundy Fritil-
  lary, 20, III
Dysstroma truncata, eggs of,
  93, *94*

Ear Moth, 59, 102
Early Grey, eggs of, *68*
Ectypa glyphica, 105
Eggs, 28, 38, 39, 40, 49, 50,
  56, 61, 63, 65, 76, 79,
  80, 82, 89, 90, *6*, *7*, *27*,
  28, *38*, *39*, *47*, *58*, *59*, *60*,
  66, *67*, *68*, *75*, *79*, *91–4*
Egg-laying, 2, 8, 9, 16, 19,
  23, 32, 38, 65, 83, 99,
  100, *1*, II
Electrophaes corylata, *82*
Elephant Hawk-moth, 63,
  66, *42*, VII
Emeralds, 98
Emperor Butterfly, 37, *31*
Emperor Moth, 59, 87, 88,
  69, *70*, X

Endromis versicolora, *71*
Engrailed Clay, 80
Epirrhoe alternata, 99
Epirrhoe galiata, 99
Erannis marginaria, *85*
Erannis defoliaria, 100
Erannis leucophaearia, 100
Erebia aethiops, 31, *27*
Erebia epiphron, 31
Eriogaster lanestris, 90
Erycinidae, 20
Erynnis tages, 35
Essex Skipper, 35
Euchloë cardamines, 12, *10*,
  11, II
Euclidemera mi, 105
Eulype hastata, 98
Eumenis semele, 32, V
Euphydryas aurinia, 19, 20,
  III
Euphyia bilineata, 99
Eupithecia centaureata, 98
Eupithecia venosata, 98
Eupithecia pulchellata, 98
Euproctis chrysorrhaea, 75,
  76
Euproctis similis, 74, 76
Everes argiades, 28
Eyed Hawk-moth, 63, 66,
  43, *45*

Fabre, J. H., 74, 76, 89
"Father of the Village", 67
Fan-foot, 59
Feathered Gothic, 80, VIII
Fertilisation (of eggs), 50
Five-spot Burnet, 105
Footman Moths, 96
Forester, 105
Foxglove Pug, 98
Fox Moth, 87, 90, 91, *59*
Fritillary, 19, 20, 37, 38,
  51, *20*, *21*, *33*, III, VI

Garden Tiger, 93, *74*, VIII
Gastropacha quercifolia, 91,
  92, 93, *77*, *79*
Gatekeeper, 31, V
Gem, 102
Genital organs, 50
Geometridae, 97, 100
Ghost Moth, 103
Goat Moth, 104, *95*
Gold Swift, 103
Gonepteryx cleopatra, 10
Gonepteryx rhamni, 9, *2*, *3*,
  4, *5*
Gothic, 80
Graphiphora augur, 80, 81
Grass Eggar, 90
Grass Emerald, 98
Grayling, 32, V

Greasy Cut-worm, 83
Green Archer, 79
Green Hairstreak, 23, *23*
Green Pug, 98
Green-veined White, 13,
  48, II
Grey Dagger, 81, VIII
Grey Arches, 79
Griposia aprilina, 79, *62*, *63*
Grizzled Skipper, 35, *29*
Gynandromorph, 25

Hadena cucubali, 80
Hadena lepida, 80
Hadena serena, 80
Hairstreaks, 23, 39, 41, *23*,
  24
Hamearis lucina, 20, III
Hausmutter, 82
Hawk-moths, 63–9, 116,
  42–50
Heath Fritillary, 20, *21*
Heart and Club, 80
Heart and Dart, 80
Hedge Brown, 31, V
Heliothis armigera, 83
Heliothis peltigera, 83
Hemerophila abruptaria, 60,
  61, 102, *92*, IX
Hemaris fuciformis, 67
Hemaris tityus, 67
Hemithea aestivaria, 98
Hepialus hectus, 103
Hepialus humuli, 103
Hepialus lupulina, 103
Hepialus sylvina, 103
Herald, 85
Herse convolvuli, 68
Hermaphrodites, 25
Hesperia comma, 35
Hesperiidae, 34
Hibernation, 9, 11, 26, 79,
  89, 98, 99
High-brown Fritillary, 19,
  38
Hipparchus papilionaria, 98,
  81
Holly Blue, 21, IV
Hop Dog, 74, 75
Humming-bird Hawk-
  moth, 66, *48*
Hutchinsoni, 56
Hycloicus pinastri, 68
Hygrochroa syringaria, 102,
  86–90
Hydriomene furcata, 99
Hymenoptera, 62

Ichneumon fly, 34, 62, 70,
  82, *18*, *19*, *51*, *78*
Ilse, Dr. Dora, 8, 45, 46
Iodis lactearia, 98

Isle of Wight Fritillary, 20, 20, III

July High-flier, 99

Kentish Glory, 87, *71*
Killing-bottle, 108, 109

Lackey Moth, 90, *75*
Lampides boeticus, 28
Lampra fimbria, 81, 82
Lanceolata, 31
Laothoe populi, 66, *44*
Lappet, 91, 92, 93, *77, 79*
Large Blue, 28, 29
Large Copper, 40
Large Emerald, 98, *81*
Large Heath, 31
Large Lustre Butterfly, 37
Large Skipper, 35
Large Tortoiseshell, 40, *35*
Large White, 12–17, *12*, II
Lasiocampa quercus, 89, 91, *72, 73*
Latticed Heath, 102, IX
Legs, 2, 6, 8
Lepidoptera, 4
Leptidea sinapis, 12
Leucania littorali, 83
Leucania pallens, 83
Leucania unipuncta, 83
Leucania vitellina, 83
Leucoma salicis, 77
Lilac Beauty, 102, *86–90*
Lime Hawk-moth, 66, *46, 47*
Limenitis camilla, 38, *34*, I
Lime-speck Pug, 98
Lithosiinae, 87
Little Emerald, 98
Lobster Moth, 73, *54, 55*
Lomaspilis marginata, 99
Long-tailed Blue, 15, 28
Loopers, 97
Lotus corniculatus, 23
Love-flight, 43, 46, 47, 103
Lulworth Skipper, 35
Lycaena dispar, 40
Lycaena phlaec, 40, *32*
Lycia birtaria, 102
Lygris mellinata, 99
Lymantriidae, 74
Lymantria monacha, 77
Lysandra bellargus, 27, *26*, IV
Lysandra coridon, 26, 27, IV

Macroglossum stellatarum, 66, *48*
Macro-lepidoptera, 60
Macrothylacia rubi, 90, *59*
Maculinea arion, 28
Magpie Moth, 59
Malacosoma neustria, 90, *75*

Maniola jurtina, 30, 31 V
Maniola tithonus, 31
Mating habits, 43–8
Marsh Fritillary, 19, 20, 107, III
Marbled White, 32, 33
Marmoris, 32
Mazarine Blue, 28
Meadow Brown, 30, 31, 33, 49, 107, V
Measuring worms, 97
Melanargia galathea, 32
Melanthia procellata, 99
Melitaea athalia, 20, *21*
Melitaea cinxia, 20, *20*
Merveille de jour, 79, *62, 63*
Methylated spirit, 108
Micro-lepidoptera, 60
Mimas tiliae, 66, *46*
Migrants, 6, 39, 67, 68, 83, 102
Migration, 13, 14, 15, 55
Miltochrista miniata, 96
Milkweed Butterfly, 15
Mimicry, 45
Monarch, 15, *17*
Mormo maura, 84
Mottled Umber, 87, 100
Mottled Willow, 83
Mother Shipton, 59, 105
Mouffet, 14
Mourning Cloak, 58
Mullein Shark, 84
Muslin Moth, 96
Mustard oil, 17

Naphthalene, 108
National Trust, 22
Narrow-bordered Bee Hawk, 67
Narrow-bordered Five-spot Burnet, 105
Neglected Rustic, 59
Net, 108, 109
Netted Pug, 98
Neuroptera, 103
Newman, L. Hugh, 14, 28
Noctuids, 50, 60, 78, 79, 80, 82, 83, 84
Nonagria typhae, 83
Notodonta dromedarius, 71
Notodonta ziczac, 71, *53*
Notodontidae, 70
Nymphalidae, 39, 43
Nymphalis io, 10, 11, *6, 8, 9*, I
Nymphalis polychloros, 11, 40, 42, 57, *35*

Oak Eggar, 61, 87, 89, 91, *72, 73*

Obsoleta, 31
Ochlodes venata, 35
Oleander Hawk-moth, 69
Old Lady Moth, 59, 62, 79, 84, 85
Operophtera brumata, 59, 100
Opisthographis buteolata, 102
Orange-tip, 12, *10, 11*, II
Orange Moth, 101, *84*
Orange Swift, 103
Our Half-mourner, 32
Ourapteryx sambucaria, 101, IX

Painted Lady, 6, 51, 55, 83, *38, 39*, I
Pale Brindled Beauty, 87, 100
Pale Clouded Yellow, 12
Pale Prominent Moth, 73, *58*
Pale Tussock, 74, 75
Panaxia dominula, 95
Papilio machaon, 22, 23, *22*
Papilio podalirius, 23
Parage aegeria, 31, *28*, V
Parasites, 17, 62, *18, 19*
Parage megera, 32, V
Peacock, 9, 10, 11, *6, 8, 9*, I
Pearl-bordered Fritillary, 19, III
Pearly Underwing, 83
Pebble Prominent, 71, *53*
Peppered Moth, 100, 102
Phlogophera meticulosa, 85, IX
Phalaena typica, 80
Phalera bucephala, 73, *57*
Pieridae, 12
Pieris brassicae, 12, 13, *12*, II
Pieris napi, 12, 13, II
Pieris rapae, 12, 13, 16, II
Pine Hawk-moth, 68
Pine Processionary, 74
Pins, 108
Phigalia pedaria, 100
Philereme transversata, 99
Philudoria potatoria, 90
Plebejus argus, 26, IV
Plusia chrystitis, 83, VIII
Plusia gamma, 81, 83, VIII
Plusia moneta, 83
Plusia pulchrina, 83
Poecilocampa populi, 80
Polia nebulosa, 79
Polia tincta, 79
Polygonia c-album, 56, *40*
Polyommatus icarus, 25, 26, 48, *25*, IV
Pontia daplidicae, 12
Poplar Grey, 81, *64*
Poplar Hawk-moth, 66, *44*

Pretty Pug, 59
Primitive moths, 103
Privet Hawk-moth, 63, 64, 65, 69, *41*, VII
Proboscis, 3, 53, 65
Procris statices, 105
Prominents, 70, 71
Protective colouring, 9, 33, 60, 80, 85
Protein, 50
Pseudopanthera macularia, 102, IX
Pterostoma palpina, 73, *58*
Pugs, 60, 98
Pupa, 1, 2, 50, 65, *67*, *71*, *72*, VII
Purple Emperor, 37, 39, *31*
Purple Hairstreak, 39
Puss Moth, 70, 71, 72, *51*, *52*
Pyrgus malvae, 35, *29*

Queen of Spain Fritillary, 15, 39, 58

Red Admiral, 6, 14, 28, 39, 54, 55, *36*, *37*, I
Red Underwing, 79, 82, VIII
Relaxing jar, 108
Rhodometra sacraria, 102
Rhopalocera, 4
Ringlet, 31, 32, 43, 48, *30*, V
Rock-eyed Underwing, 33
Rosy Footman, 96
Rush Veneer, 83
Rustics, 79, 80

Sallow Kitten, 71
Saturnia pavonia, 87, 88, *69*, *70*, X
Saturniidae, 87
Satyridae, 30, 31, V
Scarce Bordered Straw, 83
Scarlet Tiger, 95
Scarce Tissue, *91*
Scarce Umber, 87
Scent-organs, 52, 88, 103
Scent-scales, 3, 51
Scoliopteryx libatrix, 85
Scotch Argus, 31
Sesiidae, 103
Setaceous Hebrew Character, 80
Setting (of butterflies and moths), 110, 111, 112
Shark Moth, 84
Shore Wainscot, 83
Short-tailed Blue, 28
Shuttle-shaped Dart, 80
Sight (of butterflies), 3, 16
Sight (of moths), 87

Silver Cloud moth, *60*
Silver-ground Carpet, 99
Silver-spotted Skipper, 35
Silver-studded Blue, 26
Silver-washed Fritillary, 38, *33*, 51, VI
Silver Y, 81, 83, VIII
Silvery Arches, 79
Skippers, 3, 34, 51
Small Blue, 26, IV
Small Copper, 40, *32*
Small Eggar, 90
Small Elephant Hawk-moth, 66, *42*
Small Heath, 31, 49
Small Mountain Ringlet, 31
Small Pearl-bordered Fritillary, 19, VI
Small Skipper, 35
Small Tabby, 59
Small Tortoiseshell, 5, 6, 7, 9, 46, 51, I, *1*
Small White, 12, 14, 15, 16, II
Smell, 3, 87, 88
Snout Moth, 59
Span-worms, 97
Speckled Wood, 31, 32, *28*, V
Speckled Yellow, 102, IX
Sphingidae, 63
Sphinx ligustri, 63, 64, 65, 77, *41*, VII
Spinach Moth, 99
Spilosoma lubricipeda, 96
Spilosoma lutea, 96
Spinneret, 2
Spring Usher, 59
Spurge Hawk-moth, 68
Stauropus fagi, 73, *54*, *55*
Stridulation, 11
Striped Hawk-moth, 116
Strymonidea w-album, 39, 41
Strymonidea pruni, 39
Super-cooling (protection from cold), 115
Swallow-tail, 22, 23, *22*
Swallow-tailed Moth, 101, IX
Sweet Gale Moth, *66*
Swift Moths, 103
Sycamore Moths, 80

Tawny Shears, 80
Temperature, 50
Ten-o'clock Sleeper, 105
Thecla betulae, 39, *24*
Thecla quercus, 39
Theria rupricaria, 100
Tholera popularia, 80, *67*, VIII

Thorn Moths, 102
Thymelicus acteon, 35
Thymelicus lineola, 35
Thymelicus sylvestris, 35
Tiger Moths, 93, 94, *74*, VIII
Tongue, 59, 63, 68, 78
Tortrix viridana, 59
Transformation, 8, 9 (cf pupa and chrysalis)
Tracing-paper, 108
Triphaena comes, 82
Triphaena janthina, 82
Triphaena pronuba, 81, 82, VIII
Triple-spotted Clay, 80
Turnip Moth, 80
Tussocks, 70, 74, 76, 77, *56*

Underwings, 79, 81, 82, VIII
Unicorn Hawk-moth, 68

Valezina, 38
Vanessa atalanta, 6, 14, 28, 39, 54, 55, *36*, *37*, I
Vanessa cardui, 6, 51, 55, 83, *38*, *39*, I
Vapourer, 76

Wainscots, 79, 82
Wall Butterfly, 32, 46, 47, 49, V
Warning colours, 61
Waved Umber, 60, 61, 102, *92*, IX
Waves, 60
Weather, effect of, 49
White Admiral, 37, 38, 39, *34*, I
White-bordered, 58
White Ermine, 96
White-letter Hairstreak, 39, 41
White Satin Moth, 77
Whites, 12, 13, 14, 43–6, 48, *12*, *13*, *14*, *16*, II
Winter Moth, 59, 87, 100
Wood White, 12

Xanthoroë montanata, 99
Xylocampa areola, 68
Xylomiges conspicillaris, *60*

Yellow Shell, 99
Yellow-tail, 74, 76
Yellow Underwing, 78, 81, 82, VIII

Zygaena filipendulae, 104, 105
Zygaena lonicerae, 105
Zygaena trifolii, 105